Men and Women

A History of Costume, Gender, and Power

An exhibition at the
National Museum of
American History
Smithsonian Institution

by Barbara Clark Smith
and Kathy Peiss

1989

Library of Congress Cataloging-in-Publication Data

Smith, Barbara Clark,
    Men and women: a history of costume, gender, and
power / by Barbara Clark Smith and Kathy Peiss.
        p.   cm.
    ''An Exhibition at the National Museum of American
History, Smithsonian Institution.''
    Includes bibliographical references.
    ISBN 0-929847-02-4 : $6.95
    1. Costume—United States—Social aspects—
Exhibitions. 2. Costume—United States—History—
Exhibitions. 3. National Museum of American History
(U.S.)—Exhibitions. I. Peiss, Kathy Lee. II. National
Museum of American History (U.S.) III. Title.
GT605.S53   1989
391′.00973′074753—dc20   89-600244
                                CIP

*Men and Women: A History of Costume, Gender, and
Power* and the related exhibition at the National Museum
of American History were made possible by grants from
the Smithsonian Institution Special Exhibition Fund and
the National Cosmetology Association.

This publication is available from:
Publications Division—MBB66
Department of Public Programs
National Museum of American History
Washington, D.C. 20560

Other titles in the popular booklet series include:
*Engines of Change: An Exhibition on the American
   Industrial Revolution* (1986), by Steven Lubar
Field to Factory: Afro-American Migration 1915–1940
   (1987), by Spencer Crew
A Material World (1988), by Robert Friedel

(Cover): detail from ''The Discord.'' The complete image is
shown on page 9. *(Courtesy of the New-York Historical Society)*

(Title page): Barbie, about 1960. (Barbie is a trademark owned
by and used under license from Mattel, Inc.© Mattel, Inc. 1989.
All rights reserved.) G.I. Joe, about 1974. (G.I. Joe is a registered
trademark of Hasbro, Inc. © 1989 Hasbro.)

ACKNOWLEDGMENTS

A generous grant from the National Cosmetology Association has made possible both this book and the exhibition that it accompanies—"Men and Women: A History of Costume, Gender, and Power"—at the National Museum of American History (NMAH), Smithsonian Institution. We are grateful to them for the enthusiasm and support that they have provided throughout several years of work on these projects.

This book grows out of the "script," or wall text, for the exhibition. The close relationship between this publication and the exhibition means that many people have contributed, directly or indirectly, to the following pages. James Sims, who designed the exhibition, has been essential to its conceptual development. Members of the Costume Division at NMAH—Barbara Dickstein, Shelly Foote, Karen Harris, Claudia Brush Kidwell, and Carol Kregloh—have been an important source of information about costume history. Research done under their auspices and published in *Men and Women: Dressing the Part*, edited by Claudia Brush Kidwell and Valerie Steele, has particularly informed the exhibition. Shelly Foote and Claudia Brush Kidwell also read early versions of the script and offered helpful criticisms, corrections, and suggestions. Other readers of the preliminary exhibition script include Barbara Melosh of NMAH and George Mason University and Barbara Schreier of the University of Massachusetts at Amherst. Their comments have improved the exhibition and book alike.

We have many people to thank for the compelling photographs and graphics in the pages that follow. Susan Walther brought creativity and energy to the project of designing this book. The fine object photographs are the product of her efforts and of photographer Dane A. Penland's skill and dedication. Together, Susan and Dane have made the photographs both imaginative and right. Karen Harris prepared costume objects for photography, overseeing their conservation, mounting them on forms, and advising on their appropriate presentation. Shelly Foote researched graphics and secured negatives and permission for their use from various historical repositories. We are also indebted to Camilla S. Clough, Collections Manager for "Men and Women," who coordinated photographic work; Robert Selim, who edited the book; and Eleanor Boyne, for her support and assistance throughout this project.

Finally, our thanks to Daniel Bluestone and Philip S. Krone for their salty commentary.

BCS
KLP
Washington, D.C.
Lido Beach, Fla.

CONTENTS

7   Introduction
Who Wears the Pants?

11   **Making a Difference**

25   **The Strenuous Ideal**

33   **The New Woman**

51   **The Moderns**

63   **In Our Times**

77   Notes

79   Bibliography

Who Wears the Pants?

Whatever differences nature has made between the sexes, society creates many, many more. Scholars often use two different terms to make this point. They carefully distinguish ''sex''—meaning the biological natures we are born with—from ''gender''—meaning the characteristics that we take on as we learn to be ''masculine'' or ''feminine'' as our society defines these ideas. The distinction between sex and gender, or natural and social differences, is a crucial one, in

Men's razors, toiletries, and shaving equipment from the 1860s to the 1950s.

part because every society casts its own particular and historical ideals as ''natural,'' claiming that changing those ideals of masculinity and femininity would be impossible or wrong.

Historically, of course, concepts of men and women, masculinity and femininity, have changed. Equally important, however, when ideals for gender roles have remained the same over long periods, they have been held in place by powerful pressures of socialization. What often appears to be ''natural'' activity is actually the result of socially constrained choices.

This book approaches the history of gender by examining social rules for dress and appearance in the American past and present. As the title suggests, it is a history of costume, but that does not mean merely a history of clothes. Clothes, after all, are made to be worn on specific social occasions by living, moving, feeling human beings. They are not made to be displayed (as they often need to be in museums) on motionless mannequins. How people have worn their clothes, how they have shrugged their shoulders, pocketed their hands, fluttered their fans, sat in long skirts, walked in high boots, arranged their hair, or groomed their faces—all these are intrinsically part of the real history of costume. This book examines many aspects of the history of appearance, of which clothing itself is only one important part.

Appearance is a complex thing—at once trivial and vitally important. We know or believe that our looks do not express our essential selves; many of us would say that, fundamentally, a person's looks just don't matter. Yet the energy that so many of us invest in appearing right, the time and money we are willing to spend, the discomfort we are willing to undergo, all suggest that looks—and the social rules that govern them—matter a very great deal in American culture.

These rules frequently appear arbitrary when viewed from a historical or cross-cultural perspective. We can see that there is nothing intrinsically masculine about pants, for example. In many cultures and at many times, women have worn them and seemed feminine. In this sense, the symbolism of the garment in Western history—its association with men—is simply random. Yet that does not make the social rules for such garments insignificant. Any man who doubts the power of those rules can test them by seeing what happens when he wears a skirt. The reality is that people who break the rules face embarrassment, humiliation, and often social ostracism. Powerful social pressures make us conform.

One measure of the power of learned ideals is the lengths to which individuals have gone in an effort to fit or approximate them. To look ''right,'' Americans have padded out or corseted in their bodies. They have worn clothing cut to produce the fashionable shape of their times. They have shaved, plucked, and decorated their faces. They have worn boots and shoes that add height and—especially in the case of women—tilt their bodies forward and produce stilted ways of walking. They have exercised and starved themselves to build up fashionable muscles and to shed unfashionable flesh. For most of American history, women have been expected to pay more attention to their appearance than men. (This book devotes more pages to women than to men in an effort to explain why that has been so.) But as an array of products promising to prevent baldness or restore thinning hair would show, men have also worried about their looks.

Cultural ideals have been generated, disseminated, and rendered compelling in different ways over the past two hundred years. People have learned about fashionable appearance and proper behavior from numerous sources. The most powerful have included nineteenth-century magazines, the theater, photographs, the movies, and, after World War II, television.

Despite their pervasiveness, cultural ideals for masculine and feminine appearance do not have unlimited power. Some Americans of different regions, classes, or races have held divergent ideas of how to look. Although some people have curled their hair, straightened their noses, or bleached their skin, many others have taken dominant ideals for appearance much less seriously. At times, groups that have dissented from the dominant culture have made their own alternative ideals broadly felt. An example is the power of the "Black Is Beautiful" movement of the late 1960s, which affected dominant white notions of beauty as well as expressing the ideals of many African Americans.

The power of cultural ideals over individuals varies too: Some people devote more time, money, and attention to appearance than others. Still, cultural ideals of one sort or another do influence everyone. Different generations align their bodies and distribute weight on their feet differently as they learn the "proper" posture of their era. Social rules for posture get right down to the bone. Even the naked body, which seems natural, is the product of history and culture.

This study asks two questions that uncover the historical quality of things that are often considered "natural": How have appearance and

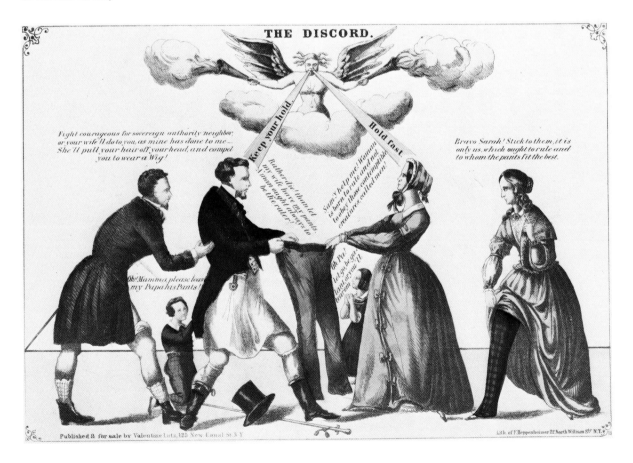

"Rather die! than have my wife have my pants. A man ought always to be the ruler!" "Woman is born to rule and not to obey those contemptible creatures, called men."
"The Discord," a print published in 1855, offered a satiric comment on the controversy over women wearing bloomers, a form of pants. *(Courtesy of the New-York Historical Society)*

fashion come to be the particular concern of women? How have muscular bodies and strenuous physical activity come to be particularly associated with men? In exploring these questions, we trace important moments in the growth of these ideals of masculinity and femininity.

And what do these ideals mean? In this book, we try to understand the power and tenacity of the social rules for male and female appearance by uncovering their links to other social rules for male and female behavior. It is not merely that there have been ''proper'' ways for men and women to cross their legs, smoke a cigarette, or groom the faces they see in the mirror every morning. It is that these rules—and the hundreds of others that we learn growing up—carry a broader social significance. There have always been links between how men and women are supposed to look and how they are supposed to live their lives, just as there have been connections between rules for appearance and the different opportunities, activities, and rewards available to women and men. There are links between appearance and power. When people ask ''Who wears the pants?'' they are recognizing these historical links.

A brief study like this one can address only a handful of topics in American history, and because it treats the time span from 1780 through the 1980s, its approach is episodic. Although this work picks out particularly significant themes, it is far from a complete or final history of appearance and gender. It deals much more fully with the ideals and experiences of middle- and upper-class white Americans, the groups most studied by costume historians, than with other groups. Working-class immigrants and Black Americans appear in these pages, but scholars do not yet know enough about their behaviors and ideals. Historians are only beginning to explore the relationships between rules for appearance and the social construction of masculinity and femininity. It is our hope that this book will stir its readers to consider these relationships and, in so doing, open up new possibilities for understanding who we are and who we can become.

Long hair on a woman's head has been considered her ''crowning glory,'' but hair on other parts of her body has been another story.

(Right) An embroidered waistcoat (1780s), silver buckles, silk stockings, and lace ruffles were all gentlemen's finery in the eighteenth century.

MAKING

A

DIFFERENCE

A mericans of the 1700s followed conventions of dress and appearance that clearly set off men from women. Women of all classes wore skirts, while men generally wore pants—either breeches to the knee or, among men in the laboring classes, long trousers. Upper-class women, at least, wore "stays," corseting that constricted their waists and produced what was considered an attractive feminine shape, while men did no such thing. And there were countless other differences in hair styles, shoes, hats, and various other accoutrements of dress as well.

Yet eighteenth-century Americans did not observe conventions that later generations would come to consider natural. Thus, upper-class women and men alike wore colorful, luxurious fabrics, silk stockings, lace, embroidered garments, and jewelry. There was nothing "feminine" about these things. No one considered it odd or effeminate for a gentleman to wear ruffles on his shirts, to fasten his stockings with decorative garters, or to wear shoes adorned with silver buckles. Well-to-do men worried about being "in fashion" just as women did. Virginia gentleman George Washington instructed a buying agent in London that "whatever goods you may send me, let them be fashionable, neat and good of their several kinds."[1] Making a fine figure on important social occasions was part of Washington's

The gentleman of the 1780s: silk coat, breeches, and embroidered waistcoat, 1770–1780; knee buckles set with paste stones, 1780–1799; the shirt, cravat, and shoes are reproductions.

The lady of the 1780s: brocaded silk gown, 1775–1780; the hair ornaments, ruffles, and petticoats are reproductions. (Research for both of the mannequins under the direction of Claudia Brush Kidwell.)

gentlemanly role. Reaching that ideal required more than the right clothing. Men as well as women might study with tutors or dancing masters to learn how to stand, gesture, sit, and move in ways that seemed graceful and genteel. Both sexes consciously aspired to beauty, elegance, and social polish.

Clothes and appearance mattered so much in eighteenth-century America because they played a great part in setting the well-to-do and socially prominent apart from the rest of society. The deportment, elegant style, exacting standards of grooming, and luxurious clothing of rich men and women clearly marked them off from their social inferiors. As little as 1 percent of their society's population, wealthy merchants, slaveholders, land-owners, and professionals and their families made up a class that was small but conspicuous. Their clothes

proclaimed their eminence in a variety of ways. The expense of the materials they wore placed their standard of dress far beyond the reach of most Americans. The fashionable skirts of wealthy women, for example, required yards of expensive fabric and distinguished them from poorer women, who wore simpler skirts of cheaper fabrics. A man's lace, silk gloves, or fine fabric for an embroidered waistcoat were also costly imports. People of the middling and poorer sort might sometimes afford a silver button or two, but only the wealthiest Americans could array themselves in finery from head to toe.

It seems likely that the clothing of the well-to-do hung differently on their bodies, too— that it simply fit them better—for it

**Our land free,
our men honest,
our women fruitful.**
A popular colonial toast

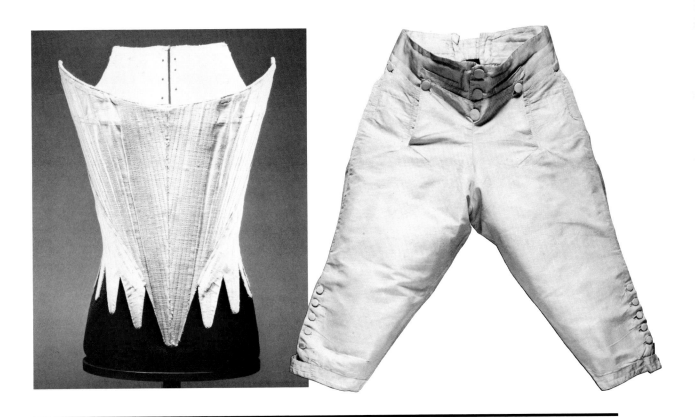

In the eighteenth century, a woman's stays constricted her waist into the conical shape considered attractive then.

Gentlemen of the eighteenth century wore breeches like this silk pair from the 1770s, while men of lesser rank wore long pants.

14

homemade clothing, cut, fitted, and stitched by women working within their households. And while many Americans could afford some imported, store-bought materials of middling or lesser quality, a good many wore clothes of homespun—that is, fabrics woven by American weavers from the wool or linen yarn spun by women and children on American farms. A quick glance told an observer the social class of a man or a woman. As it had been for centuries, costume was an emblem not only of gender but of wealth and social position.

Men Unadorned

By the 1840s, however, gentlemen no longer wore powdered wigs, tight-fitting breeches, silk stockings, colorful fabrics, laces, or buckles on the shoe and on the knee. Only their waistcoats were made with patterned fabrics. Many colors and ornaments were now associated only with women. In a sense, men abandoned color and adornment in appearance and replaced it with neutrality and restraint.

Why did this change occur? How did we come to a world in which concern for appearance is considered particularly feminine? The reasons are complex. We know that some people in England and America had long preferred "plainness" in dress. Members of the Society of Friends, or Quakers, were known for their simple clothes, for they consciously rejected the powdered wigs, bright ribbons, gold and silver buckles, and other luxurious items that established wealth and social standing in the seventeenth and eighteenth centuries. Although they rarely went so far in opposing social hierarchy and luxury, other religious groups in America shared the Quakers' prejudice against "extravagant" fashion. Yet if these ideas were familiar and widespread, they quite clearly carried little weight in the lives of the

was made to measure for them and designed, cut, and sewn by trained tailors and dressmakers who followed the fashions of London. A few wealthy Americans even kept their measurements on file with an English tailor and paid for the latest styles to be made for them and shipped across the Atlantic. Many others relied on the skills of artisans who practiced in American cities and patronized barbers and hairdressers, wigmakers, hatters, shoemakers, and jewelers, as well as tailors and dressmakers. Cheaper tailors and leather dressers provided clothes for urban dwellers of lesser rank and fortune— shopkeepers, artisans, and sometimes laborers. Yet most Americans of the eighteenth century wore

Elegance was still important to the gentleman of the 1840s, but he avoided the color and ornament favored by his counterpart of the 1780s. Suit coat and black beaver hat, about 1842; the shirt, vest, and cravat are reproductions.

English aristocracy and gentry or those well-to-do Americans who imitated them. Besides, Quakers preferred plain dress for men and women alike. And what is striking about fashions of the 1840s is that only men, and not women, abandoned color, ornament, and individuality.

In both England and the colonies, some fashionable men began to adopt plainer dress beginning in the 1760s, developing a more restrained look appropriate to "country gentlemen" rather than aristocratic members of the royal court. The American and French revolutions contributed to this trend, since both attacked aristocratic pretension and linked "virtue" and "patriotism" with plainer dress. Since only men enjoyed political rights and the status of "citizens" in these republics, perhaps it seemed particularly appropriate that they abandon aspects of dress and demeanor associated with monarchy and aristocracy. Ideals of the republican citizen, a man associated with industry and simplicity rather than leisure and ornament, contributed to the change in male costume.

Equally important, the emergence of radically new rules for male appearance accompanied the emergence of a new organization of society. As America industrialized, a new and growing middle class replaced the eighteenth-century gentry as cultural leaders. A middle-class man worked in a profession or in the new offices of mercantile and industrial America. His subdued, three-piece suit reflected and reinforced his social role: He was not an aristocrat at leisure but a hard-working, self-

Charles Oakford's Hat Factory, about 1850; Charles Oakford and Sons Hat Store, about 1860. *(Courtesy of Atwater Kent Museum and The Library Company of Philadelphia)*

"Obviously the connection between dress and war is not far to seek; your finest clothes are those that you wear as soldiers."— Virginia Woolf. This helmet of the First City Troop of Philadelphia, 1840s, illustrates the point.

16

disciplined man, daily meeting the responsibilities of the marketplace. For middle-class gentlemen, then, "masculinity" became associated with a new and different set of attributes.

Men's fashions still changed from year to year, but they changed much less dramatically than women's did. Novelty, individuality, and "fashion" became considered "feminine." The uniformity and stability of middle-class male dress expressed some of the values prized in the male business world, where reliability and self-control were more important than flamboyance or individuality.

Of course, men still paid attention to fashion, and they still tried to distinguish themselves from those below them on the social scale. The middle-class gentleman prided himself on the quality of the fabric used in his suits and the precision of the cut rather than on silver buttons or other adornment. Impeccable grooming, spotless white collar and cuffs, and a skillfully tied cravat all helped to identify a wealthy man as prosperous and genteel.

A good custom tailor was still important to achieve this ideal, for only skilled design, cutting, and sewing could produce the exacting fit that fashion required. Yet as the nineteenth century wore on, growing numbers of office workers and professionals—men whose salaries would not stretch to pay for expensive cloth and expert tailoring—desired genteel clothing as well. To meet the demand, tailors adopted proportional sizing systems that allowed them to extrapolate the dimensions of an entire suit from only a few measurements of a man's body. They developed standardized patterns and hired semi-skilled sewers at low rates to do some of their work. These changes made it possible to produce affordable clothing for the growing middle class. Men could buy these "ready-made" clothes rather than the more expensive made-to-measure. As a result, men ranging from lowly clerks to aspiring professionals could buy relatively similar, respectable suits "off the rack." Before the Civil War, suits were available in a range of fabrics and sizes and at a variety of prices, all of them cut to the fashionable shape of the era.

By the 1840s, then, many men had adopted a fashionable, middle-class "look." In workplaces like Oakford's hat store, the owner of the shop was surrounded by clerks who dressed very much like him. Dressing like the boss expressed something about the status of the clerk's job. "Clerk" was an entry-level job in the early 1800s.

The expanding ready-made clothing industry made it possible for men of many different incomes to purchase fashionable clothes in the nineteenth century.

Some men who started out in that position might hope to learn the business and move up. And almost all who worked in that position cared about distinguishing themselves from the working-class men below them.

For their part, working-class men—artisans and workers—wore different clothes and often held different ideals for how they should look. On the city street, soft-collared shirts made of sturdy, colored fabrics and ruggedly made trousers marked off artisans and workers from the middle-class gentlemen above them. In Oakford's hat factory, the workers' clothes—rolled up sleeves, sturdy work apron—contrasted sharply with their employer's business suit. The idealized artisan pictured in engravings of the period had a brawny chest and strong arms and looked very different from the small-waisted, elegant gentleman shown in "fashion plates." But while all men did not look alike or wish to do so in the 1840s, a good number did dress uniformly—as middle-class men, common (if not quite equal) participants in the male world of business and political affairs.

There remained a few exceptions. First, in one part of the male world—the military—uniforms retained the colors and decorative elements eliminated from the business suit. Self-assertion, individual valor, and other traits prized by an older, aristocratic ideal seemed appropriate to military life. Second, a small number of the urban poor "dressed up" to their social betters in expensive and showy clothes. Lower-class dandies such as the "Bowery Boys" of New York City copied and caricatured the traditional dress of the upper classes. As middle-class men dressed in darker and darker colors, with

> **With her heart on her lips and her soul in her eyes—What more could I ask in dear woman than this.**
>
> **Godey's Lady's Book, 1846**

greater and greater modesty, it was members of the "lowlife" such as the Bowery Boys who retained older conventions of conspicuous colors, fancy silks, and laces.

For the most part, however, these aspects of dress had been identified as feminine by the 1840s—certainly within respectable middle-class society. Perhaps the most important aspect of the transformation in men's dress was the way that it set middle-class men apart from women. For, by comparison, women's appearance changed relatively little from the eighteenth to the nineteenth centuries. Of course, clothing *styles* altered radically. But women of the nineteenth century still corseted their

The ideal of "true womanhood"—embracing piety, purity, and domesticity—was conveyed by the clothing and stance of this 1840s lady. Dress, bonnet, collar, broach, and parasol, 1840–1844.

bodies, wore long skirts of lustrous fabrics, and adorned themselves with flowers and jewelry. Women simply did not adopt plainer dress. While middle-class men's fashions varied less from year to year, middle-class women aspired to the latest styles from Paris. People came to think of "fashion" as something that only women worried about.

Fashion's Place

These dramatically new rules for male and female appearance accompanied the development of new roles for men and women and the elaboration of new beliefs about male and female nature. In the 1700s, men and women had both worked in the household to produce food, cloth, and many other goods. In the 1800s, production slowly moved out of the home and men went off to daily employment in offices, factories, and stores. Middle-class women still worked at household tasks, but their work became more invisible to men. People came to see women as the "leisured" and "decorative" sex.

Correspondingly, it became essential to men's identity that they were not just distinct from but opposite to women. By disassociating themselves from color, ornament, and fashion, men made their differences from women more pronounced.

In advice manuals, magazines, and novels of the era, writers articulated a social ideal to describe and direct women's lives. Increasingly, people saw "work" as something that took place outside the home. They spoke

Milliner's head, 1840–1860, used to display caps and bonnets.

of the home as a refuge where women should use "superior morality" to uplift, educate, and civilize men and children. Looking beautiful was part of the role of providing men with a restful and refining haven from the harsh business world. Beauty could help take men's minds from the competition of business and politics and lead them to morality and tender emotion. Beauty, in other words, was part of a woman's duty.

These ideas had important consequences for women's lives. From childhood, a girl learned what counted as "beautiful" in her society. One source for these standards of appearance were women's magazines, such as *Godey's Lady's Book*, which circulated widely among middle-class readers. The typical heroines of magazine stories and the models pictured in fashion plates were short, small-waisted, and slender in form. They had fine white hands, little feet, and delicate facial features. Magazine writers associated these features with a woman's character: A small mouth, for example, denoted freedom from strong passions, while large, expressive eyes supposedly reflected inner depths, and a pure complexion represented purity of soul. The male heroes of magazine stories did not receive such detailed physical description.

While many cultural sources provided a single, clear, fashionable ideal—implying that all women should try to attain one attractive look— women were still supposed to appear "individual" in ways men were not. The middle-class man picked out a ready-made suit at an urban store and felt appropriately dressed at a social occasion when other men in attendance were wearing roughly the same thing. By contrast, a woman paid dressmakers to give her a distinctive, personal look that fell within the guidelines of current fashion but set her apart from other women with whom she socialized. Women needed to find the time to buy fabric and attend dressmakers' fittings or (if they could not afford that) to do their sewing for themselves. Supposedly free from the demands of work, women were expected to spend time and attention on appearance and fashion as men were not.

Of course, enhancement and display of the body could be a source of pride and pleasure for a woman. But it also meant seeing herself through other people's eyes, defining her worth according to her success at pleasing men. The fashion-conscious woman faced a dilemma: She learned that it was her obligation to care for her looks and—in a world where marriage was the main career open to women—to attract men. But she might also find herself ridiculed for too much concern with appearance and artifice. "Fashion" was required of women, but it was also taken as a sign of their "frivolity," "vanity," and even "dishonesty."

There were other problems inherent in the middle-class domestic ideal of the nineteenth century. Although Americans associated "femininity" with physical delicacy, limited abilities, and restricted activities, the reality was far different. Women performed strenuous activity inside and outside the home in the 1800s. Most middle-class women worked hard managing their households. Even women who had servants planned and cooked meals, cleaned house, sewed clothing, raised children, and organized a thousand details to keep their homes running smoothly. Working-class women did heavy work as domestics, laundresses, and mill workers. Southern slave women toiled in cotton fields alongside men. In all these jobs and situations, women were expected to wear skirts, as if assuring the world of their essential femininity even while their actions disproved the stereotype. The middle-class domestic ideal ignored the physically taxing nature of much women's work. Those who viewed women as the opposite of men simply had to ignore many realities of women's lives.

The Corset

Other rules for appearance and dress distinguished between the sexes as well. The overall shape of fashionable clothing did not set men and women apart in the 1840s. An hourglass shape—rounded shoulders and hips accentuated by a small waist—was considered proper for both. Gentlemen and ladies trained themselves to stand in the correct posture and use appropriate gestures in order to attain the fashionable shape. But there the similarity ended. Males and females achieved comparable silhouettes in very different ways. Women created an hourglass figure by wearing constricting undergarments, while men's look was built into their clothes by skillful tailoring. Men wore padded coats to create an illusion of broad chest and shoulders and to create fullness below the waist. Women wore laced corsets that bound their waists and pushed their flesh upward. Women's clothing was more restrictive, both physically and symbolically, than men's.

Corsets had existed for centuries, taking different forms as fashion dictated different ideal shapes for the female body. Starting about 1820, corsets particularly constricted the waist, giving their wearers the fashionable hourglass silhouette. Most women of most classes wore corsets. Few laced them so tightly as to cause pain, although the constricted waist did cause discomfort for many. But it

That man . . . says that women need to be helped into carriages, and lifted over ditches, and to have the best place everywhere. Nobody ever helps me into carriages, or over mud puddles, or gives me any best place, and ain't I a woman? . . . Look at me! Look at my arm! I have plowed and planted, and gathered into barns, and no man could head me—and ain't I a woman? I could work as much and eat as much as a man (when I could get it), and bear the lash as well—and ain't I a woman?

Sojourner Truth, an ex-slave, 1851

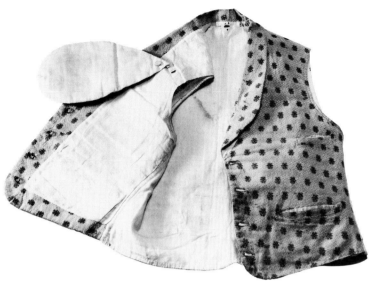

was considered unfashionable and even "immoral" to go without a corset in the 1800s. Indeed, people came to describe a woman's moral character by reference to her corsetry. "Loose" women, a term used in the eighteenth century for those who wore their stays unlaced, were sexually promiscuous. "Straight-laced" women were proper and even prudish, their bodies inaccessible and tightly under control.

Contemporary medical theories also urged women to wear corsets. Doctors and other experts claimed that women's bodies were too weak to go without support. From girlhood women learned that corsets made them more marriageable and more attractive. Making a smaller waist was part of a woman's duty to enhance her appearance and could provide the satisfaction of helping a woman fit her culture's ideals of beauty. Corsets, in other words, managed to be both respectable and sexy.

While women laced their corsets in order to appear small-waisted and busty, men donned padded clothes to achieve the body shape shown in contemporary fashion plates. Women and men both learned proper ways to stand and gesture from fashion plates. Vest with padding, 1825–1835. Corset, 1880s. Men's fashion plate, 1841.

Still, a minority of men and women opposed the practice of corsetry. Health reformers argued that corsets deformed a woman's body. Feminists argued that women's constricted waists symbolized their social and sexual repression. The practice of corsetry, they said, reinforced men's idea that women were primarily sexual beings. Some men ridiculed corsetry as evidence of women's vanity and over-concern with fashion and appearance. In the 1890s, social critic Thorstein Veblen compared Western societies' use of corsets to the Chinese practice of binding young girls' feet to keep them small. Both practices, said Veblen, were "mutilations of unquestioned repulsiveness to the untrained sense. It requires habituation to become reconciled to them." But it was not just that many people had become accustomed to corsets, Veblen concluded. Corsets worked to underscore the twin associations between men and work, women and physical incapacity. A corset, Veblen wrote, "lower[ed] the subject's vitality and render[ed] her permanently and obviously unfit for work."[2]

Skirts, Pants, and Bloomers

Corsets were not the only aspects of early nineteenth-century fashion that limited women's physical freedom. The tight, sloping sleeves on dresses of the 1840s restricted a woman's arm movements. Throughout most of the century, too, women faced the burden of heavy skirts that both inhibited movement and symbolized physical inactivity.

How did women come to be restricted to skirts? In some cultures, pants and skirts are not symbolic of gender at all. In China, for example, members of the elite mandarin class wore flowing robes, so that skirted costumes, not pants, became

associated with prestige and power. Pants were something that peasants, male and female, wore. They became emblems of lowly social status.

In the West, pants and skirts have had a different history. In medieval Europe, feudal lords and ladies both wore long, flowing robes. Trousers were worn by soldiers and others—male or female—who rode horseback. But by the 1400s, only men wore pants. They had become emblems of masculinity and authority, while skirts were associated primarily with women. By the 1800s, Americans thought of these conventions as natural and timeless.

Skirts were not always symbols of subservience even in the West. In the 1800s, middle-class men wore long gowns as ministers, judges, and professors. These skirted costumes were symbols of honor and accomplishment in occupations considered

21

Advertisement from the *Delineator*, October 1909.

peaceable and contemplative rather than vigorous or athletic. Long, flowing garments were worn by men who functioned outside what was seen as the harsh, masculine world of politics and the marketplace. Women were largely excluded from these occupations and from the "skirts" worn in them.

One other fact illuminates the meaning of pants and skirts in America. Dresses were associated with young children of both sexes as well as with adult women. Until the late nineteenth century, boys and girls under age four or five both wore dresses. Infants of either sex might wear embroidered garments and frilly or lacy bonnets. These things were not merely "feminine." They symbolized their wearer's exclusion from the privileged world of mature, male adulthood. Boys put aside dresses for breeches as their first step toward manhood. Girls would stay in skirts throughout their lives.

By the 1840s, even on those occasions when women took part in the same activities as men, pants were forbidden to them. Middle-class ladies' most strenuous leisure activity was horseback riding. Convention required ladies to ride sidesaddle rather than astride like men. Sidesaddle riding was seen as an opportunity to demonstrate feminine virtues—grace, beauty, and control though gentleness rather than command. The female riding habit was, of course, skirted—sometimes dangerously long in order that a woman's legs and ankles be fully covered when she sat sidesaddle on the horse. A "lady" should care as much about modesty as safety.

Not everyone was happy in the prescribed life or the prescribed dress of a "lady." In the 1850s, feminists proposed a form of trousers for women: the bloomer. For these women, the bloomer represented both greater freedom of movement and freedom from traditional limitations on women's role. In devising the bloomer, dress reformers drew on their period's interest in "Oriental" styles of "Turkish trousers" and on their experience as children. Little girls had worn pantaloons and shorter skirts for several decades. Reformers also modeled the bloomer on a form of exercise dress that a few women had been wearing in private since the 1830s.

Many people agreed that women's fashions needed reform. Long skirts made it difficult to garden, do housework, or even walk the street. A

Bustles made of wire or fabric could be attached to a lady's waist under her skirt to accentuate her posterior. Silk padded bustle, 1885–1895; woven wire bustle, about 1885; bustle of buckram tubes, 1897–1900.

number of doctors, educators, women novelists, advice writers, and social reformers urged women to ignore the dictates of fashion and adopt more "rational" dress. But of course women were also strongly urged to remain "feminine" and fashionable. Only a very few women ever wore the bloomer costume in public in this period. Those who did met with public ridicule and often private ostracism. Opponents argued that bloomers were indecent and unhealthy and that women who wore them were trying to become like men in the social arena. People associated bloomers with radicals who advocated women's rights. An outraged *Harper's Magazine* put it in 1857, "We believe in the petticoat as an institution older and more sacred than the Magna Carta."[3] The angry, threatened reaction of the majority of people to the bloomer underscores the profound identification of men's and women's appearance with their expected gender roles. People thought the skirt was necessary if women were to remain in their role as "ladies," apart from the world of business and politics. As dress reformer Mary Tillotson succinctly observed, in the public mind, "Pants are allied to Power."[4]

Men in dark suits, women in colorful skirts—these images are still familiar today. We still follow some rules for male and female appearance that Americans followed in the 1840s and before. But other rules—that pants are only for men, for example—have changed.

Most people assume that their culture's conventions are "natural," so that change seems impossible or wrong. But in many periods, some people, like the bloomer reformers, have been uncomfortable with the rules they inherited and have seized the opportunity to depart from the conventions of their times. As the continuing story of the bloomer suggests, it has often been easier to

stretch the rules in private than in public. As the rest of this book will show, most change has been in one direction: Women have frequently adopted a garment or a style detail that was previously associated with men, while men have rarely appropriated a feature of feminine appearance. For most of the period since the 1840s, it has seemed essential to most men to distinguish themselves visually from women; men's appearance changed as they felt challenged by women and others in the late nineteenth century.

23

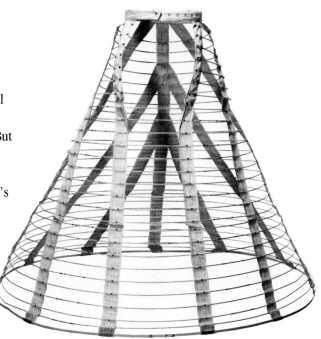

Wire hoops created a fashionable bell shape in the 1850s and 1860s. Hoops helped ladies maintain physical distance and social propriety. *(Courtesy of the National Park Service)*

24

BLOOMER COSTUMES OR WOMAN'S EMANCIPATION.

Women who wore the bloomer costume were subjected to ridicule and caricature in the 1850s. This print depicts dress reformers in male stances and with cigars, riding crops, and other symbols of masculinity. *(Courtesy of the Harry T. Peters "America on Stone" Lithography Collection)*

(Right) Muscles and masculinity: turn-of-the-century baseball shirt, football shirt, Indian clubs, dumbbells, and popular sports cards—all signs of the new importance of sports in defining masculinity.

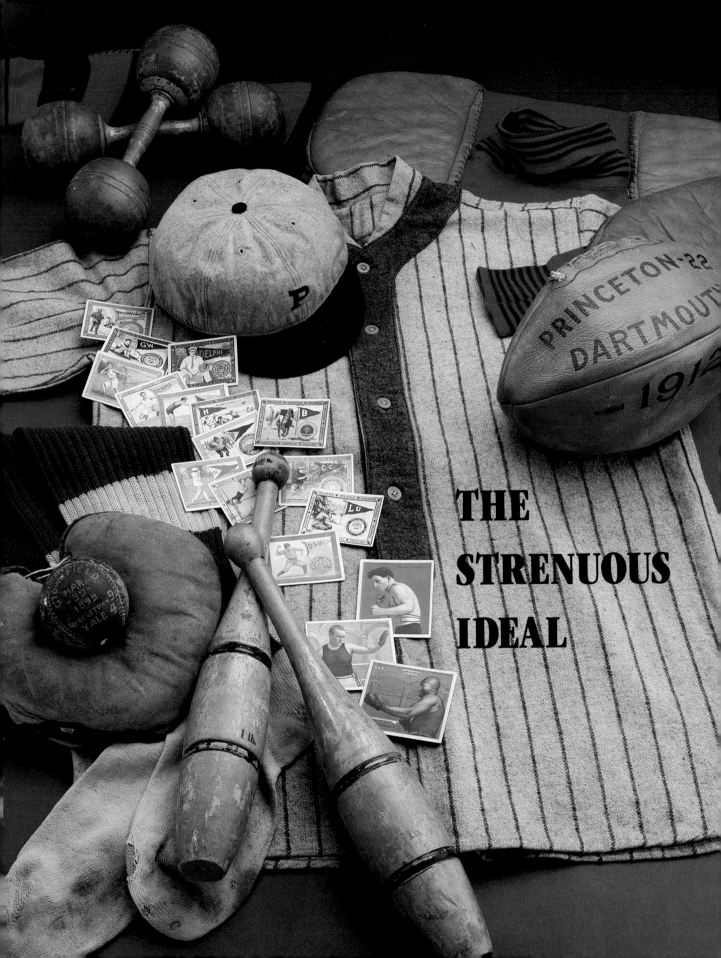

THE STRENUOUS IDEAL

By the end of the nineteenth century, the "elegant gentleman" of earlier decades had become a fop. Cartoonists lampooned him as an un-American aristocrat, a dandy, and a dude. To wear a monocle in one's eye, protect one's hands with gloves, and carry a gold-headed cane all came to seem overly fastidious, fussy, and unmanly. The older style of business dress—long frock coat, high collar, stiff-bosom shirt—suddenly seemed affected.

Beginning in the 1880s, the more formal clothing of the gentleman began to give way to a looser and more casual suit. The new sack-type business suit eliminated the "skirts" of the frock coat. Worn with softer shirts and low collars, the sack suit created the illusion of a solid, muscular body within. This became the standard uniform for increasing numbers of middle-class men working in white-collar office jobs.

There were other changes in appearance, too. Fashionable men became more clean-shaven, often keeping a mustache but less often wearing a beard or heavy sideburns. Men had been shaved at barber shops for some years, but by the turn of the century, manufacturers of safety razors and shaving cream were urging men to shave themselves. The clean-shaven face, their advertising stressed, offered a youthful, go-getter appearance.

Beyond the change in men's dress and grooming, middle-class men in the 1880s and 1890s adopted a new image of their bodies. Rejecting the ideals of masculine appearance that had prevailed early in the century, they began to prize muscular bulk rather than leanness, physical strength rather than genteel weakness. New figures emerged in the popular culture—the cowboy, boxer, and football player—who represented these ideals. Men increasingly identified masculinity with muscularity and sought to live "the strenuous life."

Men and Muscles

The vogue for muscles can be seen in the craze for exercise, calisthenics, and weight-training, a movement that gained sharply in popularity after the Civil War. Gymnasiums sprang up in many cities. Here men exercised on mats and bars and worked out with dumbbells and Indian clubs to increase upper-body strength and develop a symmetrical torso. They practiced leg-lunging routines for lower-body strength. Men's clothing was easily adapted for exercise. In the mid-nineteenth century, men wore loose-fitting trousers, and, in the privacy of all-male clubs and gymnasiums, they might do without shirts altogether. By the end of the century, they often wore specialized knit garments that allowed them a full range of movement unencumbered by excess fabric.

Youth magazines and organizations such as the Boy Scouts of America and the YMCA urged boys to exercise. Physical and moral training could mold boys into strong and patriotic young men. Ernest Thompson Seton put it this way in the 1910 *Handbook* of the Boy Scouts of America: "Realizing that *manhood*, not *scholarship* is the first aim of education, we have sought out those pursuits which develop the finest character, the finest physique, and which may be followed out of doors, which, in a

Tailor's display figure, made of metal with painted upper body, 1874–1890.

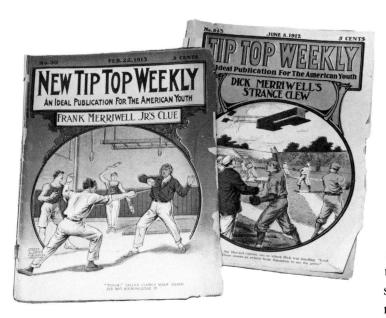

managerial positions might learn quick decision-making from football. And on the playing field, the sons of old wealth and the sons of new wealth could learn to compete and cooperate together.

The violence of early football drew criticism from educators, doctors, and the general public. In the 1890s, schools outlawed the dangerous flying wedge, and players began to wear canvas jackets, nose and shin guards, pants with cane reeds at the thighs, and padding for protection. But for some fans of the game, violence was what made football a "masculine" game. Contemporaries drew analogies between warfare and football, and between football and "primitive life." Perhaps padding found acceptance because it served two purposes: While it protected a player's body, it also exaggerated his male musculature.

While upper- and middle-class men played football at college, working-class men enjoyed the game as well. Workers did not need to worry about losing physical toughness from too much leisure or sedentary white-collar work. But they did find their work less meaningful as employers introduced machinery, rendered older skills obsolete, and increased their vigilance over workers' use of time on the shop floor. For working-class men, sports represented a freer arena where a man's individual skills still counted. Like middle-class men, workers enjoyed football and connected skill at the game with manliness. (But no one suggested that their skills at football fitted them for managerial positions in corporations or government!)

In the 1860s and 1870s, baseball appealed to craftsmen and workers, who associated skill, discipline, and training with "manhood" at their work and play. Promoters turned it into a professional sport which drew thousands of

word, make for manhood.''[5] By linking physique and manliness, Seton expressed ideas that grew more and more common in the early twentieth century.

Colleges, too, fostered the new masculine ideal. For most of the nineteenth century, colleges had educated well-to-do men to be teachers, ministers, and men of letters. Now they became training schools for the future leaders of new corporate and government bureaucracies. Many schools changed their curriculum to fit this new purpose—dropping Latin and Greek in favor of history, literature, and other liberal arts. Sports also became a central part of education at many colleges in the late 1800s.

Alumni, coaches, and physical educators argued that it was less important to teach a set body of knowledge than to teach hard work, efficiency, and cooperation. "Manly sport"—football, track and field, rowing, boxing, tennis, golf, gymnastics—might promote the college man's "will to win." Football, many believed, could socialize young men in the values of teamwork and aggressive competition. Men who would later work in

Were American boys becoming milquetoasts and sissies? *Tip Top Weekly* and other magazines taught them competition and courage.

28

spectators to watch its artistry. Middle-class men took up college and amateur baseball. Although not as rugged as football, baseball still became tied to masculinity. When women in a few women's colleges tried the game, experts disapproved, insisting that it was simply too strenuous for females. When male players began to use gloves to protect their hands, some fans worried that the game was becoming less manly.

Boxing was another sport that achieved greater popularity late in the century. Boxing required courage, strength, and skill—qualities

Survival of the fittest: ruggedness on the football field became an ideal of American college men in the 1890s.

Quilted football pants, 1905.

Bare-knuckle boxer John L. Sullivan was the most widely known American athlete of the nineteenth century. He won and wore this championship belt.

central to working-class ideals of masculinity throughout the 1800s. Middle-class men, committed to steady habits and sober self-control, generally disapproved of boxing. They disliked the violence of the sport and the boisterous crowds of gamblers and lowlife that surrounded it. But late in the 1800s, more and more middle-class men became attracted to the spectacle of two boxers in combat. Fighters seemed to exhibit the aggression and physical power appropriate to a more "manly" and "primitive" world.

In the 1880s, new rules barred wrestling holds and throws, added gloves, and set up regular, three-minute rounds and rest periods. These changes did not make boxing much safer, and fighters continued to come from working-class backgrounds. But the new rules made boxing more respectable. Equally important, the fight ring moved inside sporting arenas. By charging for tickets and controlling crowd behavior, promoters kept out "undesirables" and made the prize fight a respectable mass entertainment. Some middle-class men boxed as amateurs and much greater numbers attended professional bouts. Although spectatorship did not build muscles, men enjoyed a break from work and a chance to exercise their emotions and imaginations by viewing a "manly" contest.

The Middle Class Unmanned

Why did football and other vigorous sports figure so much in men's definition of masculinity? The vogue for muscles was one response to a growing fear that middle-class men were becoming weaker. More and more Americans lived in cities, and city life seemed to pose threats to health and vigor. This seemed a particular problem for youth: Middle-class city boys might grow up as "molly coddles," "pussy-foots,"

or "sissies." For their part, middle-class urban men increasingly performed white-collar jobs and lived sedentary lives. Men suffered from nervousness, indigestion, and a host of other disorders attributed to city life and sedentary "brainwork." Doctors, ministers, and educators encouraged physical activity to counteract the killing pace and wearing routine of work.

According to experts, the problem was not simply that the work of middle-class men was difficult and draining. Equally important, that work had lost much of its meaning. Men of the 1800s learned to take a sense of manliness from working hard at their jobs and providing economic support for their wives and children. But economic and social changes made it more and more difficult for many to take satisfaction from the work itself. After the Civil War, a few men built large corporations and amassed fortunes, while most men had to abandon their dreams of economic independence. Most would never own businesses of their own or rise to become partners in large firms. Even prosperous, middle-class men would live their lives as the employees of others. Towering figures such as John D. Rockefeller, Cornelius Vanderbilt, and J.P. Morgan made it harder for ordinary men to feel successful.

Patent medicines of the turn of the century promised to restore men's physical strength, vigor, and sexual prowess. Shown here is N.K. Brown's Iron and Quinine Bitters.

Men also felt threatened by women's changing roles. Since masculinity had so long been defined in contrast to ideas of femininity, women's increasing efforts to win education, employment opportunities, and political rights also affected men's ideas about their bodies, their appearance, and their identities. Their sense of manliness depended on feelings of superiority over women, and most sought to keep women out of colleges, voting booths, and careers. As growing numbers of women entered the workplace, work was less clearly essential to determining masculine identity. If women were workers—and at times actually competed with men for jobs—what defined manhood? As a bastion of male exclusivity and an arena of manly self-assertion, sports was one answer to the crisis in masculinity. As *Independent Magazine* put it in 1909: "The football field is the only place where masculine supremacy is incontestable."[6] This statement revealed a profound anxiety, however. How essential, after all, was the football field to modern life?

In the 1890s, another image of manliness—far from the daily grind of office and shop—caught the imagination of Americans: the cowboy. Real cowboys were working men, hired hands of the cattle industry that boomed in the West between 1866 and 1886. The *idea* of the cowboy caught the imagination of many eastern and urban Americans. In dime novels of the 1890s, the cowboy became a symbol of the tough, laconic loner, living a rugged life away from cities and civilization. Through books and, in later years, movies and television, men could temporarily escape to the frontier, a place of freedom, youth, and male companionship. In their imaginations, they could leave behind the demands of maturity: the daily grind at office or factory; responsibilities to women, children, and the home; and the need for self-discipline and control.

In life as in a football game . . . hit the line hard!

All the great masterful races have been fighting races.
Theodore Roosevelt

The idea that a "strenuous life" was essential to manhood found its most famous supporter in Teddy Roosevelt. Sickly as a boy, Roosevelt built up his body through a rigorous exercise regimen. He took boxing lessons, mastered horseback riding, and became a skilled marksman. Besides holding political office, in the course of his life he ran a cattle ranch, fought against the Spanish in Cuba, and shot wild animals in Africa. He associated all of these activities with manliness, an

Army recruiting poster, 1914.

ideal that combined physical strength, prowess, and moral character.

Roosevelt encouraged every young American boy and man to live "a life of manly vigor." He also associated manliness and militarism. He pushed for the United States to build up its naval power to compete with other empires of the world. He supported U.S. seizure of American Indian lands, Cuba, the Philippines, and Hawaii and urged intervention in Central and South America. He believed that white people—especially Anglo-Saxons—were superior to other "races," whom whites should dominate and protect. A manly nation would be superior, strong, and willing to use force to defeat those who blocked its prosperity and power.

The Survival of the Fittest

These ideas resonated powerfully among many Americans. In the last two decades of the century, immigrants from countries in Central and Southern Europe began to arrive on American shores; by 1910 more than nine million had emigrated to the United States. Members of the old Anglo-Saxon elite responded with anxiety and xenophobia to these new Americans. Like earlier immigrants, such as the Irish and Germans, the newcomers met with prejudice and discrimination. Violence against Blacks in the American South also escalated in the 1890s. Some Americans worried about the dominance and purity of the Anglo-Saxon race.

Moreover, working-class activism seemed to threaten middle- and upper-class economic power and political authority. Economic depressions in the 1870s and 1890s fostered radical labor movements. Workers' protests against wage cuts and work changes met with strong—sometimes brutal—resistance by government and corporations. Bloody

confrontations between unions and soldiers or National Guardsmen took place in industrial cities and in mining and railroad towns. When the growing labor movement flexed its muscles, the middle-class's fears of its own weakness redoubled.

The natural and social sciences provided new theories that shaped the way Americans thought about strength and weakness. Perhaps the most influential theory of the period was Charles Darwin's concept of "natural selection," first proposed in his book *Origin of Species* in 1859. Darwin argued that different species of plants and animals developed their distinctive traits through natural selection. Those individuals best suited to their environments survived and reproduced, passing

Fears of radicals, immigrants, and disorder are plainly illustrated in this drawing of the 1877 railroad strike. Images like this fueled middle-class men's preoccupation with physical strength and combat. (*Courtesy of the Library of Congress*)

on their successful traits to their offspring, while less hardy individuals perished.

In the late 1800s, many Americans applied Darwin's ideas to the lives of men and women in society. This stream of thought placed great value on physical strength and vigor and reinforced men's preoccupation with manliness. Living in a competitive, capitalist society, Social Darwinists argued that the essence of life was struggle. Individuals, races, and whole societies had to compete to survive, and their superiority and inferiority depended on their fitness in the struggle. Social Darwinist ideas provided people with ways to

diagnose the problems that middle-class men faced at the end of the century. According to some, men were becoming over-urbanized, over-refined, over-civilized—in a word, unmanly.

In the face of armed conflict, racial and ethnic tension at home, and warfare abroad, physical fitness seemed vital to middle-class men. Sports became a training ground for the militarism and national assertion of the age. Even the modern Olympic games, created in 1896 to encourage athletic competition and sportsmanship among nations, can be seen as a response to these concerns. The Olympics allowed men to act out the struggle between nations on the terrain of sport. The early Olympics permitted only men to compete; only gradually did women win inclusion in most swimming, gymnastics, track-and-field, and other events. Representatives of their countries, the finest of young men, Olympic athletes embodied the ideals of manliness and national power so prevalent in this period.

In the late nineteenth century, the playing field became central to men's lives, both actually and figuratively, by linking athleticism and physical development with social, economic, and political power. As articulated by Teddy Roosevelt and others, this ideal tied ''manliness'' to physical strength and combat, metaphors for ways that men should look and behave in every arena of life. New standards for male appearance allowed men to assert their strength and aggressiveness far from the playing field. If few men played football, especially after college, many could adopt a clean-shaven look that seemed both vigorous and boyish. In the workplace, too, men wore the ''sack-type'' business suit that bespoke their athleticism and physical strength. The strenuous and muscular ideal had become the hallmark of middle-class masculinity.

The sack suit had a short jacket and voluminous cut. Compared with the wasp-waisted gentleman of the 1840s, this image suggests a more substantial physique. Illustration from *Modern Fashions* magazine, July 1904.

(Right) This mannequin's cycling bloomers, shirtwaist, and bicycling gaiters are reproductions of originals from 1895. She rides a woman's drop-frame bike from the 1890s.

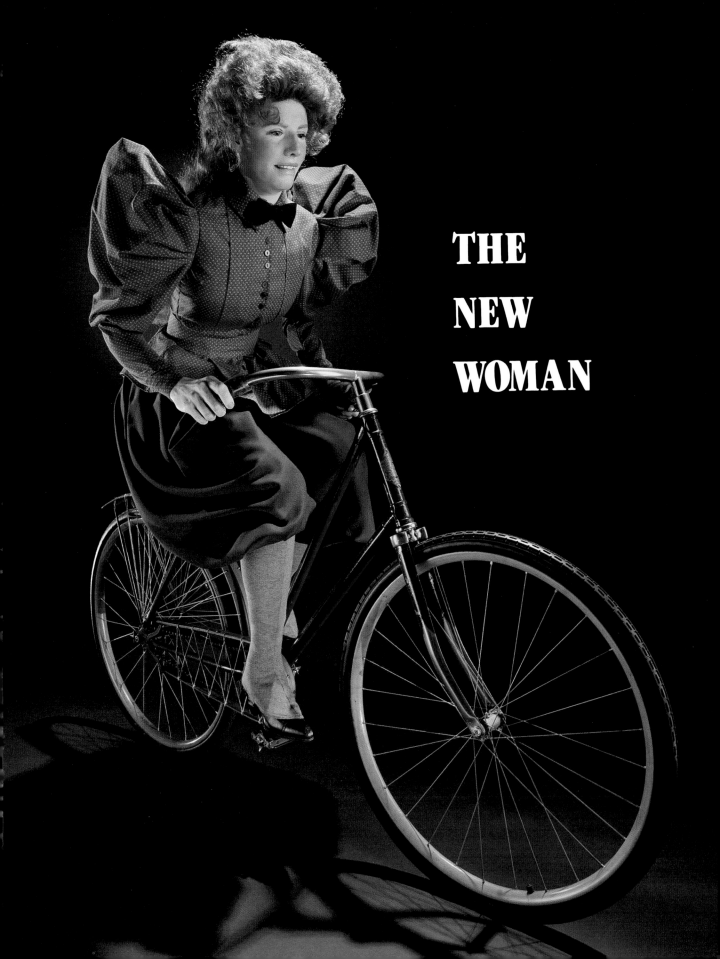

THE
NEW
WOMAN

In the late nineteenth century, the movement of women into education, work, and politics challenged the idea that women should be confined to the domestic sphere. In the decades after the Civil War, middle-class women organized and joined clubs, charity organizations, temperance societies, and other groups for education and reform. Women's colleges such as Smith and Vassar and the new coeducational land-grant universities made higher education available to a growing number of their daughters. Some women went into the professions, breaking long-established barriers in medicine, journalism, the ministry, and higher education. By the 1890s, a revived suffrage movement was gaining new adherents to its program for civil and legal rights, eventually resulting in passage of the Nineteenth Amendment, which secured the vote for women. Working-class women, too, were experiencing important changes in their lives. While wage-earning women in the nineteenth century typically worked as domestic servants, mill workers, and agricultural laborers, by the late 1800s new job opportunities were appearing for typists and secretaries, salesclerks, waitresses, and factory workers in consumer industries.

Women were newly visible: haranguing men in public meetings over the evils of drink; jostling other commuters to catch the streetcar to work; bicycling for pleasure in a public park; clambering over tenement rooftops as public health nurses. As writer Margaret Deland observed, this was "a change in the feminine ideal," from the domestic, self-effacing, and passive True Woman of yesteryear, to the "New Woman."[7]

Americans were undecided as to who this New Woman really was. Many felt threatened by the expansion of women's

THE NEW WOMAN should use the new soap—COPCO—the perfect soap. Sold by all dealers 5 cents a cake. Made only by The N. K. Fairbank Company, Chicago, New York, St. Louis.

How did manufacturers sell soap at the turn of the century? Some used the flirtatious poses of the American Girl on their packaging, while others played with the mannish image of the New Woman.

34

activities and accused women of "unsexing" themselves, abandoning their true roles as wives and mothers. One newspaper, the *New York World*, raised this issue by printing likenesses of twelve famous "new women" of the era, then drawing features from each to make a single, "composite" face. "It will be seen at once that the composite woman has a strong face. It is an intellectual face, and—it is said with some regret—possibly a stern, unyielding face."[8] Would a man wish to marry such a woman, asked the *World*? Others worried about a question that the *World* did not raise: Would an educated woman able to support herself wish to marry a man?

But the caricature of the New Woman as "mannish" was accompanied by another image, the "American Girl." Immortalized by illustrator Charles Dana Gibson, she was a young, energetic, independent, and sensual woman. Her mental and physical freedom made her appealing to women. Men liked the idea that her physical vigor was aimed at making her more attractive to them. This beautiful "New Woman" was depicted at sports, at college, in shops and parks, but rarely at work or involved in political reform movements.

In the debate over the New Woman, the female body itself became a contested issue: What was its relationship to woman's nature? How should it be used and adorned? Who should define and control it?

Physicians, scientists, and other experts argued that women were by nature delicate and dependent creatures ruled by their reproductive organs. It was, Dr. M. L. Holbrook observed in 1870, "as if the Almighty, in creating the female sex, had taken the uterus and built up a woman around it."[9] The physiological processes in women's lives—puberty, menstruation, childbirth, menopause—were considered draining, dangerous experiences that demanded a retiring domestic life. Since motherhood was women's primary duty, no activity should be allowed to jeopardize their reproductive health. Women who used their minds or sought roles outside the home, physicians observed, were likely to develop neurasthenia, a nervous disorder that made them unfit wives and mothers.

Display head, used to show wigs and hairpieces, 1880–1915.

Many women turned to patent medicines to combat female complaints associated with reproduction. This is a bottle of Dr. Simmons' Squaw Vine Vegetable Compound, late nineteenth century.

These views buttressed opposition to women's higher education, employment, and athletics. Opponents of female academies and colleges, for example, argued that if adolescent girls spent their "limited energies" on studying, their bodies would degenerate. Educated women would become sickly, unattractive to men, and produce only "puny" and "enfeebled" children. These worries grew as more white, middle-class women chose to remain single, delay marriage, and limit the number of children they bore. Heightened fears about the growing numbers of foreign-born in the United States led some people to accuse these women of causing "race suicide" and the collapse of Western civilization.

Feminists and women reformers argued that women were physically and mentally capable of taking on roles outside the home and raised a fundamental question: Who should control women's bodies? Many of them fought in the late 1800s to win married women the legal right to own property and keep money they earned by their own labor. They fought for women's custody rights over children they had borne. And they argued that women should be able to choose motherhood and avoid pregnancy for physical or psychological reasons of their own. The movement for "voluntary motherhood" insisted on the right of wives to say no to their husbands' demands for sex. Other women fought the sexual double standard and the physical abuse of wives and children. In all of these goals, women were seeking control over their own bodies.

Calisthenics were popular among both women and men, but men were allowed more freedom of movement in their clothing and the exercises they performed. Illustrations from Simon D. Kehoe, *The Indian Club Exercise* (New York: Peck & Snyder, 1866).

The Strenuous Ideal for Women

One of the ways women redefined themselves in the late nineteenth century was through exercise and sports. Supporters of exercise had urged women to improve their health with exercise since the early 1800s, but most experts said women were too delicate for much physical activity. Exercise, they claimed, would destroy women's rounded curves and make them too thin, or else make muscles too big, powerful, and ugly. In either case, women who exercised would lose their womanly charms. Advocates of exercise did not deny that women existed to attract men and bear children, but argued that exercise enhanced a woman's beauty and would help them have more and healthier offspring.

Exercises were recommended for health, beauty, and grace, rather than for strength. Before the Civil War, women were limited to walking, riding, and mild calisthenics. Exercises for ladies and girls were to be done in the privacy of the home or supervised at a female academy. Women were barred from such ''masculine'' sports as rowing and running, which emphasized endurance and competition.

The idea of women playing sports and exercising their bodies continued to shock many people in the late 1800s. Physical strength, prowess, and self-confidence clashed with contemporary notions of femininity. However, the growth of women's athletics was spurred in the 1870s and 1880s by the advent of women's colleges. Countering the charge that education made women weak and

Women enjoyed the freedom and competition of basketball, even playing by restrictive girls' rules. Inside a college or private gymnasium, bloomers seemed appropriate dress. These young women are playing at Western High School in Washington, D.C., 1899. *(Courtesy of the Library of Congress)*

sickly, Vassar, Smith, Mount Holyoke, Wellesley, and other women's colleges made training in rhythmic gymnastics or calisthenics an integral part of their curricula. College women needed to prove that they had the physical stamina to withstand the rigors of academic life.

What would women wear while exercising? Any vigorous exercise required a woman to step out of the fashionable and constricting clothing that marked her as a respectable woman. Nineteenth-century American society had been based on the separation of feminine and masculine spheres of life, and the fashionable woman's costume signified her restricted place in this social order by restricting her physical movement. When women began to exercise and play sports, people worried

that they were abandoning their duty to appear pretty, ethereal, and dependent. Bloomers, short skirts, and other clothes that would allow free movement struck many people as indecent and inappropriate.

The earliest styles of exercise clothing emphasized freedom of upper-body movement and loose-fitting waistlines. Hemlines generally fell to just above the ankles, and women were advised to remove most of their petticoats. By the 1850s, the skirts were shortened to mid-calf with bloomers worn underneath. Within the confines of women's colleges and athletic clubs, women experimented with new sports attire. By the 1900s and 1910s, women exercised in middy blouses and bloomers. The evolution of the gym costume reflected a change in exercises, too. Before the 1850s, female calisthenic programs concentrated on upper torso movements. Women used Indian clubs, dumbbells, wands, and beanbags to improve coordination, encourage graceful movements, increase flexibility, and tone muscles. Only men did leg spreading, knee lifting, and lunging exercises. When women began to add these to their athletic repertoire, the bloomer—once reviled as too radical and unwomanly—became the preferred style.

By the 1890s, college women had turned from calisthenics to basketball—a man's game. With its open competitiveness and fast pace, basketball threatened to undermine women's health and "docile femininity." In response to these concerns, physical educators in 1899 created new rules to transform a man's sport into a woman's game. Women's rules divided the court into three sections, assigned players to each section, and required a player to pass the ball to a teammate after only three dribbles. These changes reduced physical exertion and encouraged teamwork. For roughly the next

38

These women's biking pants from about 1900 were fully cut and heavily pleated to simulate a skirt. The pants are courtesy of the Valentine Museum.

seventy years, women and men played different versions of the same game.

College women wore bloomers when playing basketball indoors, but when the game was played outdoors or in front of male spectators, propriety required a change in costume. Players donned skirts instead of (or over) their bloomers. Wearing skirts to play basketball reminded women that how they appeared mattered as much as how well they played.

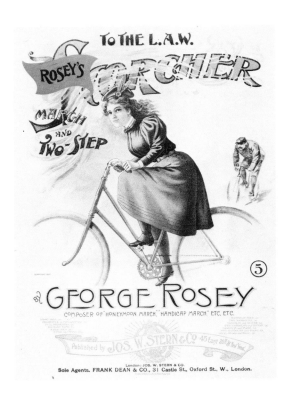

Propriety on Wheels

The question of what women should wear when exercising in public emerged especially when the

bicycling craze swept America in the 1890s. Women eagerly sought to ride the "wheel." Cycling was a middle-class sport that involved far more women than horseback riding or college calisthenics and basketball. Not confined to the private spaces of upper-class athletic clubs or the sheltered walls of educational institutions, the female cyclist was mobile, independent, and highly visible. She symbolized women's movement into the public sphere.

Women wore a range of outfits for cycling: shortened skirts over knickerbockers, divided skirts (sometimes pleated to simulate a round skirt when standing), and "Syrian trousers" that reached to the ankle. A brave minority even wore the bloomer costume, but controversy raged over those who wore pants in public. Women on bicycles in bloomers or other trousers seemed threatening in part because people connected these costumes—and athleticism in general—with the feminist movement. Women on bikes were doing more than simply exercising: They came to represent an entirely new attitude toward womanhood. Cyclists *moved*, where once women had been restricted by clothes and custom to the confines of the domestic sphere. They rode astride, pumping their legs just like men and breaking a rule that women horseback riders had accepted for generations. On wheels, women could leave the home for work or play. Little wonder that contemporaries connected bicycling, short skirts, and the possibility of gender role reversal. Popular stereocards and cartoons of the 1890s showed biking wives leaving their husbands at home with the laundry, child tending, and cooking to do.

> **'How do I look?' is the everlasting story from the beginning to the end of a woman's life.**
> *Sarah Stevenson, M.D., 1881*

The breezy image of the woman cyclist appeared on sheet music, advertising cards, and other forms of popular culture. The "Rosey's Scorcher March and Two-Step" sheet music dates from 1897.

Bicycling became socially acceptable for women, however, when elements of femininity were integrated into the activity. Most people thought it necessary for women to wear skirts while cycling to maintain their modesty and respectability. Bicycle manufacturers accommodated the skirt by adding the drop frame, making bikes less sturdy but more acceptable. In the 1890s, women who rode alone or together on a tandem bike could expect insults from men in the parks or on the streets. Dressing conservatively and having a male escort, however, reduced the risks of harassment. Thus, bicycling was most acceptable when it affirmed women's dependence on men and attention to society's rules for feminine appearance.

The bicycle craze led to the increased public acceptance of women's right to participate in sports in the late nineteenth and early twentieth centuries. More and more women put aside the idea that their bodies were fragile. Women challenged restrictions on their physical activity and often wore simpler, less constraining dress to exercise in.

The growth of athletics also offered new, acceptable occasions for women and men of the same class to socialize together. Earlier in the century, the separation of social life into domestic and public realms and stringent definitions of middle-class propriety meant that interactions between the sexes were carefully regulated. Women and men typically met at church socials, chaperoned dances, and especially in the home. By the 1890s, however, sports such as croquet, tennis, and golf permitted a new kind of social interaction for men and women of the upper class. Similarly, the development of resorts like Atlantic City and Coney Island made excursions to the beach to swim and relax immensely popular with middle-class and working-class women and men.

What to Swim In?

The greater acceptance of women and men swimming together in public, however, inevitably raised the question of women's appropriate attire and behavior. In private, single-sex settings in the nineteenth century, men could swim naked while women could swim in "Turkish trousers" or bloomers. But in public, mixed settings, there were

Bathing dress, 1898–1905. All this fabric prohibited swimming in an age when women were only supposed to splash and "bathe" in the water. The bodice and bloomers are one piece; the skirt is buttoned on. Man's two-piece linen suit, 1905–1915; boater hat 1890–1920; white canvas shoes, 1891–1910. The shirt and tie are reproductions.

strict rules for proper swimwear. In the 1830s, when mixed bathing first became popular, bathing outfits covered most of the body, whether the swimmer was female or male. Over the next fifty years, men's suits slowly shrank to allow vigorous swimming. Women's bathing costumes, however, still covered them from head to toe. In the water, the yards of fabric in these suits became so heavy that swimming any distance was impossible. Women were limited to ''bathing,'' splashing in the water assisted by men.

Why couldn't women swim? Swimming not only demonstrated and built up a woman's strength, it also required a woman to concentrate on her own activity and her own sensations. A swimmer had to think about what her body was doing rather than how she looked—thus breaking one of the primary cultural prescriptions for women's behavior. Although women could exercise in private, play sports, and ride a bicycle in public, wearing a practical, revealing suit for athletic swimming still caused debate at the turn of the century. Women's modesty and purity would be compromised by swimwear that exposed legs, arms, and torso.

ON THE BEACH

Women in long, flowing bathing costumes posed seductively on the beach in turn-of-the-century popular illustrations, like this one on a Schrafft's Chocolates Box.

Howard Chandler Christy's 1903 print of a man and woman on the beach shows how swimwear enhanced male muscularity and female appeal.

Nevertheless, Americans began to accept greater exposure of both male and female bodies after 1900. As male muscularity became the vogue, more men began to wear revealing swimsuits to show off their powerful, well-proportioned bodies. It was not until the 1930s, however, that a man could go "topless" on a public beach.

Women's suits also grew smaller to allow more athletic swimming in the early 1900s. Several women who achieved fame as swimmers popularized a more practical, one-piece suit that allowed greater mobility. Most women, however, wore stylish "bathing" suits, featured in women's magazines, rather than practical "swimming" suits. Bathing suits were designed according to fashionable conventions and reinforced the idea that women should look attractive on the beach. New, more revealing styles made some women uncomfortable, as they realized there was a fine line between enjoying the admiration of others and finding oneself the object of unwanted attention.

The exercise and athletics craze at the turn of the century undoubtedly gave women a new experience of their bodies: On the basketball court, bicycling in the park, or swimming in the ocean, women gained a new sense of physical freedom and movement. They donned clothes that, while bulky and unwieldy by late-twentieth-century standards, were looser and freer than any of the garments their mothers had worn. Although sports occupied only a small part of women's daily lives, it shaped the emergence of new cultural definitions of women. At the same time, the strenuous ideal for women could not stray too far from socially acceptable conventions of femininity. Women wearing trousers or athletic bathing suits continued to seem threatening to most Americans. The physical activity that marked the "New Woman" was acceptable as long as women remained *women*, displaying their femininity by wearing fashionable sportswear.

Modern Work and the Working Girl

Housework and childrearing continued to be the primary form of women's labor at the turn of the century, although women of different social classes experienced these in different ways. Working-class wives, for example, not only cared for their families, sometimes in unsanitary, crowded, and inefficient conditions, they frequently earned money for the

Fashion plate, 1896, *Journal des Demoiselles*. While most middle-class women followed fashion. . .

was to be emblems of wealth, displaying the conspicuous consumption of the newly rich through dress and adornment. But the typical middle-class woman was not merely a decorative doll. She *did* have a maid to do the heaviest housework, and her home typically had modern plumbing, spacious rooms, and some labor-saving devices. Even so, she worked hard, wearing a housedress of sturdy, washable fabric for much of the day. The fashionable "day dress" she put on for dinner would not suggest the drudgery of her work. Women's duty—and job—was to relieve her husband of the cares of the daily grind, not remind him that "his castle" required constant upkeep.

At the same time, the work of the middle-class woman as wife and mother was changing from that of an earlier generation. Women were increasingly consumers, purchasing a wide variety of goods and services in the marketplace. In the nation's cities, large department stores—palaces of consumption—catered to female shoppers. Social visiting and entertaining became an even more important part of the wifely role. Moreover, many middle-class women were taking part in clubs, the temperance movement, and reform. The range of activities in a middle-class woman's life is suggested by the variety of fashionable clothes she wore: cotton housedresses for work around the house; skirts and shirtwaists for shopping or meeting with other women; suits for Sunday church; dresses for entertaining; lingerie dresses for tea.

household by taking in boarders, doing laundry, or sewing garments after the housework was done.

Middle-class and upper-class women, in contrast, were often considered "ladies of leisure." Thorstein Veblen wrote in the 1890s that their role

. . .a few strong-minded women broke with convention.
Mary E. Walker, physician and suffragist, became a symbol of nonconformity when she adopted men's clothing.

Circulation Department, Correspondence Division
The Curtis Publishing Company, Philadelphia
The Ladies' Home Journal
The Saturday Evening Post
The Country Gentleman

A number of feminists, reformers, and career women wore tailored, severe suits that reflected their public roles and professional status. Some completely refused the image of traditional femininity and, claiming control over their bodies and self-image, wore trousered suits or shorter skirts in public. But most dressed fashionably, wearing conventional clothing to calm public fears about feminist demands for civil rights, education, and employment. As the suffrage movement grew stronger and more conservative in the early twentieth century, advocates argued that the vote would not cause women to abandon their domestic role; indeed, women's responsibility for protecting their home and children *led* them to support enfranchisement. Suffragists understood well the power of symbolism: Women in the massive suffrage parades of the 1910s were clad all in white and marched arm in arm, asserting their purity, morality, and solidarity as women.

Growing numbers of single middle-class women worked outside the home over the course of the nineteenth century. While some fought to enter traditional male-dominated fields such as medicine and law, many more found employment in what would become known as the "female professions"—teaching, nursing, social work, library science, and home economics. To justify their participation in the paid workforce, many argued that these jobs represented extensions of a woman's "natural" role as mother, nurturer, and caretaker. These jobs became stereotyped as "women's work."

The modern office clearly defined work roles and lines of authority. Correspondence Division of the Curtis Publishing Company, Philadelphia, Pennsylvania, about 1910. *(Private collection)*

To do these jobs, women wore variations on domestic dress. Teachers, for example, wore a version of the middle-class fashionable dress, sometimes adding an apron to it. Nurses' uniforms had starched aprons and caps and resembled maids' dress in many ways, a fact that reflected the manual labor and "housekeeping" duties of much of their work, as well as their subordinate status to doctors. However, nurses' uniforms also showed a number of fashionable touches that differentiated their dress from that of domestic servants; in the late nineteenth century, for example, they had puffy sleeves in imitation of then-current styles.

The greatest expansion of jobs for women came with the transformation of the office in the late nineteenth century. Before the Civil War, virtually all office clerks, bookkeepers, and copyists were men, but the growth of large corporations after 1865 changed the nature and meaning of clerical work. Big business required greater coordination and administration than the small offices of the antebellum period, generating enormous amounts of paperwork. Men went into the more powerful, well-paid, and promising positions of middle management while women became clerical workers. The growing acceptance of the typewriter in business also contributed to the increased numbers of women in clerical and secretarial jobs. Initially, neither men nor women were especially identified with the typewriter. Both used it, and researchers inconclusively studied which sex was better at typing. However, as women went into office work, many "experts" claimed that women's "natural" manual dexterity, their patience, and docility made them superior typists to men. Indeed, the word "typewriter" in the late nineteenth century referred both to the machine and to the woman who used it.

One clerical job still required flexibility, a variety of skills, and familiarity with different sides of a business. A "private secretary" was more likely to be a man than a woman through the 1910s. In the 1920s, women began to enter this work. As it, too, became identified with women, the private secretary came to be seen as an "office wife"—indispensable, but not a candidate for a management position.

As women moved into office jobs, social commentators raised the question of what they should wear. This seemingly trivial question was important for several reasons. Fashionable women's dress was supposed to represent their home-bound role, their concern with beauty and appearance, and their moral superiority to the values of the competitive workplace. How could women enter that workplace as efficient and businesslike workers without contradicting the idea that women were "naturally" fit for the home and unfit for the world of work? The office was even more problematic because there women would be working in close quarters with men. Cartoons, vaudeville sketches, and movies of the early twentieth century show the popular concern with flirtatious secretaries, "mashing" businessmen, and hanky-panky in the office. The proper appearance, advised women's magazines and "business girls'" manuals, could forestall such problems. Good grooming, tasteful clothing, and simple hair styles and cosmetics use were essential to feminine modesty and reserve in the workplace. "The correct business attire for the modern woman suggests the best tailoring worn by men and with just the touch of femininity which will save the woman from a certain hardness and harshness," observed the *Woman's Home Companion* in 1908.[10]

> **How a lady can make money and not lose social caste is a question of absorbing interest, but one that is seldom answered satisfactorily.**
> Harper's Magazine, *1882*

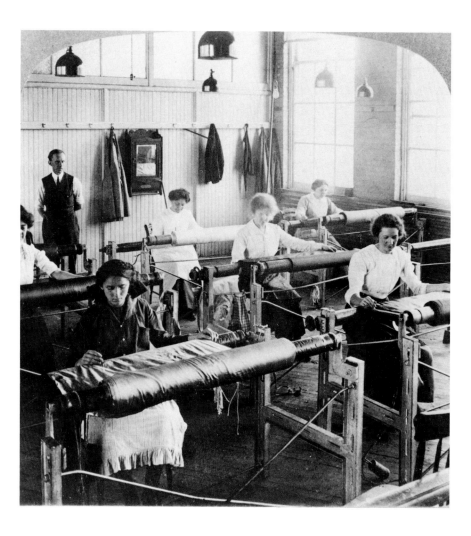

46

At the same time, being "attractive" became part of the job, especially for private secretaries. "Help wanted" ads for secretaries emphasized physical attributes and personality as much or more than ability and training. The *Saturday Evening Post* in 1931 satirized such ads by inventing a manager at an automobile manufacturing company who advertised for "an exceptionally attractive, intelligent young woman, not over twenty-five; must be educated and well-bred, with charming personality; a natural blonde, five feet eight inches tall, and slender; a smart wardrobe necessary."

The *Post* commented that the executive ordered a secretary by "laying down specifications very much as he would for a yacht."[11]

Not all women worked in offices, schools, hospitals, or libraries, however. Indeed, the vast majority of them, daughters in working-class families, labored in factories, stores, laundries, and especially in private homes as maids or cooks. Approximately six out of ten nonagricultural women wage-earners worked in domestic service in 1870. Domestic service remained the single most important

Workers "pick the cloth" on bolts of woven fabric at a silk mill in Paterson, New Jersey, 1914. While some women wore clothes that reflected their immigrant backgrounds, others adopted the shirtwaist and skirt, the "American" style. *(Underwood and Underwood Collection, Library of Congress)*

women's occupation for the next sixty years. Black became the "proper" color for domestic servants' clothing in the late nineteenth century. Maids' uniforms of economical and durable black fabrics hid stains and seldom needed to be replaced. Worn with a starched apron and cap, they conveyed an image of servility. Despite the growing number of women domestics in the period from 1870 to 1930, women workers increasingly resented "service," likening it to a form of slavery. Their uniform symbolized to them their lack of personal freedom and leisure. Domestics worked long hours and were on call all day, required to obey the commands, however whimsical, of their mistresses. They were often barred from receiving visitors, even in the kitchen, and usually were given only Sunday afternoons and Thursday evenings off.

By the 1890s, more and more young working-class and immigrant women were turning to new jobs opening up in factories and stores. Women had been among the first factory workers in the United States; when the textile mills at Lowell, Massachusetts, opened in the 1820s, "Yankee girls" from New England farms ran the spinning frames and looms. Through the 1800s, however, many industrial jobs became men's work only. Men dominated mining, construction, transport, and heavy industrial production. In the late nineteenth century, women factory workers tended to be concentrated in consumer-oriented industries, such as textiles, garment-making, food processing, cigar-making, and commercial laundering. There they worked in low-paying jobs as semi-skilled machine operators and manual workers. Around 1900, as corporate managers introduced new machines and production processes, women moved into jobs opening up in the chemical, electrical, printing, food, and metal industries. Rarely did they work alongside men, however. Even when the two sexes worked in the

same industry—as in canneries, garment making, and metalworking—they were customarily assigned different tasks. Other women found jobs in the expanding commercial and service sector of cities and towns as department store saleswomen, waitresses, and beauticians. Women's wages remained low: Most earned one-half to two-thirds of what men earned, and few could afford to live apart from their families.

Despite long hours of labor, hazardous working conditions, and low wages, many working women at the turn of the century prided themselves on their freedom, spirit, and urbanity. The "working girl" was a cultural phenomenon, commented upon by journalists and observers, worried over by reformers. Particularly noteworthy was her sense of style. She could be seen going to work in neat shirtwaists and tailored skirts, boisterously promenading after dinner in an elaborate hat and high heels, or making an entrance at a dance hall in a sharp suit and a feather boa copied from an exclusive dressmaker's design.

The shirtwaist was among the first products of the women's ready-to-wear industry in America. It became a symbol of the "New Woman" who dressed for comfort and freedom rather than following the vagaries of high fashion. As its name suggests, the woman's shirtwaist was modeled on men's shirts and, like them, buttoned down the front or appeared to do so. This style, which drew on traditional menswear, symbolized women's presence in factories, stores, and offices. While working women wore inexpensive waists, wealthier women adopted the fashion as well, using richer fabric and ornamentation. Dressy "silk waists" were worn for formal occasions. Many buttoned up the back and adopted other traditionally feminine features, including embroidery and lace inserts. Middle-class women liked simpler, tailored waists for sports and physical activity.

48

SIZES OF WAISTS, 32 TO 44 BUST. WHEN ORDERING
STATE SIZE AND COLOR DESIRED.

201—Tailored Shirt Waist of self-figured Piqué. This material is sufficiently heavy for cold weather wear. The front displays wide tucks as illustrated, and the closing is effected visibly with pearl buttons through a box-plait. The cuffs and detachable collar of the material are neatly tucked. Plain shirt back with a plait at waist line. Long sleeves, and in white only. . . . . . **Price 98 cents**

202—Shirt Waist of Corded Madras with a black cross-bar stripe. This effective little waist will command approbation at once on account of its smart appearance. The front is tucked to yoke depth. The waist closes visibly with pearl buttons. Box-plait in back. Soft buttoned shirt cuffs and detachable stiff linen collar. The jabot shown in the illustration is not included. Can be furnished with long sleeves, and in white with black stripe (as illustrated) only. **Price 98 cents**

203—Waist of Cotton Poplin. The front of this attractive waist is handsomely embroidered in the same color as the material. The embroidery on the plastron front is particularly effective. Tucks to yoke depth appear on front and extend down the entire length of the back, simulating a double box-plait. The collar and the button cuffs are also tucked. Closes invisibly at the left side of the front. Can be furnished in white, black or champagne color. Long sleeves only. . . . . **Price $1.29**

204—Shirt Waist of striped German Flannelette. This trim waist closes visibly with pearl buttons through a box-plait in the front. Deep tucks are introduced over the shoulders to yoke depth, two of which are carried down the entire length of the front, simulating a box-plait. There is also a box-plait in back. Tie shown in the illustration is not included. Buttoned cuffs of the material and a detachable stiff linen collar. Waist can be furnished in gray ground with lavender and black stripe, also in gray with green and black stripe. Long sleeves only. . . . . **Price $1.29**

205—Shirt Waist of Poplin. The chic feature of this dressy waist is the plastron front ornamented with self-covered buttons, above which is introduced a tucked chemisette of the material. Short tucks over the shoulders both front and back provide desirable fulness. The cuffs and the attached collar are tucked to correspond. A bow tie of poplin affords a trim completion. Buttons invisibly in back. Can be furnished in black, white, wine, navy or Alice blue. Long sleeves only. . . . . **Price $1.49**

206—Shirt Waist of Satin-striped Madras with a dainty white figure. The front, where the closing is visibly effected, displays a double box-plait down the entire length, and wide plaits over the shoulders form a blouse effect below. A feature of this new Tuxedo design is the front trimming of small pearl buttons. Back is neatly tucked. Attached shirt cuffs of plain linen and detachable stiff linen collar. Can be furnished with long sleeves, and in white only. . . . . **Price $1.49**

The Waists shown on this page are READY-MADE and can be furnished only as illustrated and described. We cannot make any alterations in these garments, nor can we send samples of the materials.

The popularity of the shirtwaist was spurred by the growth of the ready-to-wear clothing industry for women at the turn of the century. Most men's clothes were store-bought by the 1880s, but the women's ready-made industry lagged behind. Many men wore similar suits, while women were expected to dress differently from one another, choosing outfits to flatter their own best features. Women's styles were complex, closely fitting the body and changing more often, so that it was harder to develop a series of standardized patterns for womenswear. Besides, the female dressmakers who made women's custom clothes were relatively cheap to hire, while the male tailors who sewed men's custom clothing were expensive. And although busy working men might have no time for tailors, women were expected to go to fittings, or, in the case of poorer women, find time to sew for themselves.

The garment industry produced ready-made clothes like these shirtwaists at affordable prices for women of all classes. Advertisement, National Cloak and Suit Company, 1908.

wives and mothers. Most women workers at this time were single and left the labor force when they married. Even with the onset of World War I, when many men left their jobs to fight in Europe, most women were not pulled out of the home and into the labor market. Rather, World War I gave women who were already employed the opportunity to move into different jobs. White women substituted for white men in iron and steel mills, metal and chemical shops, lumberyards, and glass and leather factories. Black women took over white women's jobs as

The rising numbers of working women welcomed the ready-made industry. They wanted a stylish appearance and had some wages to spend on clothing, but had no spare time to sew and too little income to hire a dressmaker. Initially the garment industry produced simple designs, such as cloaks and mantillas. By the 1890s, it had branched out into shirtwaists and skirts. With the trend toward simpler, looser dress in the 1890s and early 1900s, the industry flourished. By 1910, every article of female clothing could be purchased ready-made.

Women's wage work shaped the new gender definitions and conventions of appearance in the period from 1880 to 1920 and helped to create the image of the "New Woman." But it did not fundamentally upset the traditional role of women as

Four sisters in Abilene, Kansas, about 1910, chose varieties of "waists" for their family photograph. *(Courtesy of Shelly Foote)*

This woman worker's outfit combined fashion and practicality during World War I. Illustration from *American Machinist*, 1918.

domestics and in other service positions. Some women became streetcar conductors and railroad workers.

The visibility of women in "men's jobs" during the war did cause concern. The vision of women in factory work clothes on the shop floor troubled many Americans. A "feminine" version of overalls, one that followed the lines of current fashions for women, became popular. With the armistice, women returned to "women's work."

50

Posters supporting the war effort made women workers in pants a common image during World War I.

(Right) The modern woman's finery: pink silk teddy, 1925; sheer silk stockings, high-heeled slippers, and some accoutrements of the boudoir.

THE

MODERNS

By the 1920s, the idea of what women could do had changed irrevocably. Women had won the vote. Many of them were using their new political muscle to fight for the prohibition of alcohol, the end of child labor, and social welfare legislation. Millions of women now worked for a wage. Over one-fifth of the nation's labor force was female, and more than 23 percent of all women held jobs in 1920. Many of these continued to be young working-class daughters who turned their paychecks over to parents struggling to make ends meet. But more and more women were striking out on their own, keeping their wages and living independently, at least before they married. Women's enrollment at colleges and universities also increased, and their participation in athletics rose as well.

A phenomenon observers called the "revolution in manners and morals" accompanied these changes. New commercial sites for leisure, such as dance halls, nightclubs, amusement parks, and movies, brought women and men together beyond the watchful eyes of parents. Courtship, with its implicit expectation of betrothal and marriage, increasingly gave way to dating. Attitudes toward sexuality were changing, too—with a new recognition that women had sexual needs and desires. Efforts to legalize birth control and make divorce laws more liberal attracted public support, as well as opposition.

If the Gibson girl characterized the modern woman of the 1890s to many Americans, the most common female image of the twenties was the flapper. Boyish, angular, thin, with bobbed hair, short skirts, and a cigarette or cocktail glass in her hand, the flapper symbolized "flaming youth" and modernity. The term "flapper" referred in the 1910s primarily to adolescent working girls who relished fancy clothes and dancing. By the 1920s, it described young women of any class who embraced the

Gold sequined evening dress, 1925; gold leather and brocade shoes; feather fan; all shown on a reproduction of a store display mannequin of the 1920s. The mannequin is courtesy of the Chicago Historical Society.

modern style—a style often at odds with the traditions and beliefs of the older generation.

The Modern Style

What was this modern style? A fundamental change was a new ideal body shape and silhouette for women. The body of a nineteenth-century woman was to be curvaceous; the hourglass figure and its variations were made possible by the use of corsets that constricted the waist, bust improvers, hoops, bustles, and stiff petticoats. In the decades after 1900, this shape began to disappear, replaced by a more linear silhouette, as can be seen in the shirtwaist style. In the 1910s, new fashions from Paris accelerated the move toward straighter lines. The couturier Paul Poiret, who traveled in the United States to publicize his ''hobble skirt'' and new tube-like shapes, had a particularly important impact on popular styles. Stripped down, slimmer, and more simply cut, the new styles expressed to many American women ideals of comfort, freedom, and the possibility of physical movement.

Hemlines also began to rise in the 1910s, exposing women's ankles; in the twenties, they rose almost to the knee. For centuries, Western art and dress associated visible legs with strength and activity. Draped or skirted legs were considered beautiful, contemplative, and serene. The exposure of women's legs in the 1910s and 1920s placed a new emphasis on women's physical activity. Indeed, fashion drawings and advertisements frequently depicted women in motion, swinging a golf club or dancing. Short skirts symbolized women's entry into sports, the professions, and public life.

Exposed legs also suggested a new, active female sexuality. For decades, the skirts of genteel women had swept the street. In the 1850s, for example, women who wore skirts revealing their ankles in public were generally assumed to be prostitutes or ''loose women.'' When respectable working- and middle-class young women wore skirts just below their knees in the 1920s, many people considered the fashion erotic and daring. Some condemned it as unchaste and immoral.

53

Through the twenties, women wore pants at home and at leisure, rarely at work or around town. A variety of pants outfits gained

Advertisement, Holeproof Hosiery Company, Milwaukee, Wisconsin, about 1920. *(Courtesy of Bernard Robinson)*

popular acceptance. Some, like lounging pajamas and beach pajamas, had traditionally feminine colors and styling. Other pants, like hiking breeches and the new formal riding wear, were fashioned more like men's clothes. But women in pants *just* like men's were still socially suspect. Beginning in the late nineteenth century, male physicians and reformers associated a woman's desire to wear pants with lesbianism; fears about lesbianism increased in the 1920s as more women could choose to live alone or with other women.

The slim silhouette and short skirts required different undergarments than had women's clothing of the nineteenth century. For most of the 1800s, women had worn underwear of plain white linen, decorated at most with a little embroidery at the top of the chemise. Beginning in the 1880s, lace, ribbon inserts, and color became fashionable, suggesting that women's underwear had become a symbol of erotic attraction. The styles of the twenties seemed to bring greater freedom and comfort, and many women abandoned corsets. But the slender, straight shape and active-looking body were frequently achieved artificially, by binding and flattening the breasts with brassieres and reducing the stomach and thighs with girdles.

The popularity of silk as a fashionable fabric for underpants, teddies, slips, and stockings also reduced the bulkiness of the female shape. With shorter skirts and exposed legs, sheer silk stockings were a coveted accessory. While in the 1880s, a glimpse of a woman's ankles on a public street was considered erotic, by the 1920s, "respectable" women were exposing their calves. Old-fashioned stockings—

sturdy and opaque—gave way to perishable silk, which gave an illusion of nudity.

Who wore these new fashions? Virtually everyone. In the nineteenth century, wealthy women and many middle-class women hired dressmakers to sew the latest styles. Other middle-class women sewed their own clothing, modeled on fashion plates in *Godey's Lady's Book* and other women's magazines. But many working-class and rural women could not afford the fine fabrics and expensive ornamentation that marked the costume of the well-to-do, nor was such clothing practical to wear. The rise of the ready-to-wear clothing industry, with its new methods of mass production and distribution, made fashion available to consumers of all classes. Manufacturers quickly translated the latest styles shown in Paris and New York into everyday, affordable clothes. Sears, Roebuck and other mail-order houses offered stylish clothes of varying quality and prices in their catalogues. Department stores in cities and towns also brought fashion to middle- and working-class

Powders, creams, and other beauty products, packaged in alluring containers, came on the market in the 1910s and 1920s. These cosmetics range in date from the 1910s to the 1940s.

customers. Women learned about modern styles from shop windows, movies, and especially from mass-circulation fashion magazines filled with photographs and advertisements.

The Pursuit of Beauty

Fashion designers, women's magazine editors, models, advertisers, and beauty experts played an increasingly important role in defining womanhood to the American public. In an era when women had made notable strides in education, employment, and politics, they were urged to express their individuality and talents through their appearance. Success in the business world and in marriage depended on good grooming, stylish clothes, and a charming personality. Those who emphasized beauty as the route to success accepted that men held the power in American society, so that women needed to look attractive to them. But beauty and style, they asserted, were possible for every woman. This democratic message fit in well with the consumerist spirit of the twenties: Advertisers and retailers urged women to purchase the products that would make them beautiful, stylish, and attractive to men.

The rise of the cosmetics and beauty business from the 1890s to the 1920s reinforced these views. Beauty salons appeared in the nineteenth century in many cities as places for hairdressing, but by the 1880s and 1890s their services included facials, manicures, and massage. "Beauty culture" became a big business, catering to upper- and middle-class women who could relax and indulge in the treatments. Salons vied for the most

exclusive clientele by providing luxurious surroundings, elegant fixtures, and immaculately groomed "beauty operatives." But the pursuit of beauty was popular among other women as well. Beauty parlors appeared in the commercial districts of working-class and immigrant communities. African American women such as Annie Turnbo Malone and Madame C. J. Walker pioneered in the development of hair and skin treatments and trained thousands of Black women in beauty culture. Many of these opened beauty shops in the expanding Black neighborhoods of northern cities.

55

A revolutionary hair style appeared around World War I that symbolized the modern woman: the "bob." Throughout the nineteenth century, long, luxurious tresses had been an important symbol of femininity. The ritual of putting one's hair up in the morning and brushing it out at night was a common one for women. Those without long, thick hair frequently turned to patent products like Ayer's Hair Invigorator and the Seven Sutherland

The African American beauty industry sold face powders, bleach creams, hair straighteners, and other products to Black women, urging them to care for their looks as a sign of racial pride.

Sisters tonic to promote hair growth. Others purchased switches, braids, and hair pieces called "transformations." The flappers who bobbed their hair rejected this traditional notion of womanhood. Sneaking into barbershops for the bob (since barbers cut hair rather than dressed it), they emerged newly shorn to face an outraged public. Newspaper editors, high school principals, and parents worried over the rebelliousness and morality of the younger generation. Were young women abandoning their docile and graceful "long-haired ways"?[12] Soon, however, the fashion caught on, and beauty parlors offered permanent waves and shingled styles to produce a more elegant bob.

The visible use of cosmetics also marked the modern woman. In the nineteenth century, women used a variety of creams, lotions, and tonics for skin care, some purchased from a local druggist, others made from home recipes. At various times in the 1800s, the use of "makeup," that is, visible color, was fashionable among well-to-do women. Some, for example, enameled their faces with liquid powder and tinted their cheeks with rouge. For most Victorian women, however, "painting" was too controversial, since it was associated with prostitutes. Obvious color and artifice might suggest that a woman was promiscuous, vulgar, or lower class. Cosmetics manufacturers responded by promising that their products were invisible and natural-looking.

By the 1910s and 1920s, the cosmetics industry was selling a wider and wider range of cosmetics that visibly colored women's faces. From the world of beauty culture and salons, such entrepreneurs as Elizabeth Arden and Helena Rubinstein emerged as leaders of the industry, pioneering in the development of new makeup products and techniques. Max Factor, "makeup artist to the stars," started marketing to the general public

cosmetics he had developed for the film industry. Other manufacturers appealed to women with new packaging, selling creams and lotions in elegant sets and offering face powder and rouge in portable compacts. Lipsticks in colorful shades, eyeshadows, and mascara appeared on the market after World War I.

African American beauty culturists branched out from hair-care products to skin care and cosmetics. Some Black women of the 1910s and 1920s used skin bleaches that promised to lighten and smooth their complexions—a practice that reflected the power of the white community to set standards of beauty. But white women also bought skin bleaches and whiteners, since "white women," after all, actually have a variety of skin colors, and relatively few fit the ideal of Anglo-Saxon appearance. Equally important, beauty products and advertisements aimed at Black women expressed a sense of racial pride, suggesting an alternative sense of beauty within the African American community. Having a good appearance through grooming and dress conveyed a sense of dignity, self-worth, and respectability. Such an appearance countered the stereotypical and degrading image of Blacks held by many white Americans at this time. Moreover, the beauty business offered important job opportunities for many African American women at a time when most were limited to employment as domestic servants, agricultural laborers, and laundresses.

By the 1920s, cosmetics were an accepted, even necessary, part of a respectable woman's appearance. The use of face powder and rouge was widespread, and more daring women now wore mascara and brightly colored lipstick. Powdering one's nose in public had become a common sight, however irritating the custom was to many men. The era's growing acceptance of consumption, sexual expressiveness, and women's visibility in the public sphere—as well as the hard sell of the cosmetics companies—fostered these changes.

Depictions of the modern woman in movies and magazines—decked out in flapper clothes, bobbed hair, and lipstick—stressed her free spirit, healthy athleticism, sexual freedom, and leisure. But the ideal and reality of women's lives in the twenties were often contradictory. Women frequently worked to support themselves or their families, choosing positions as saleswomen and typists instead of more traditional jobs as maids or seamstresses. Most worked until they married, but some—especially Black and immigrant women—needed to earn an income after marriage as well. Young women often found themselves doing housework, cooking, and laundering for themselves, or if they lived at home, caring for siblings. Others

were busy studying in high school and college.

Yet the popular image of women *did* reflect the desires and dreams of many. Whatever the varied demands of family, work, and school, young working-class and middle-class women relished their leisure time and opportunities to socialize with their peers. Dancing, swimming, motoring, and going to the movies, they helped to set a new and modern style of dress and behavior in their everyday lives.

Freedom to Dance

A dance craze swept America in the 1910s and 1920s. It brought growing numbers of young women and men out of their "separate spheres" and into a new, mixed-sex realm of commercial leisure. In the

The dance, the clothes, the makeup, the legs—all shocked polite society but became widely accepted anyway. This photographic still is from the movie *So This Is Paris*, 1926.

process, it fostered new cultural definitions of gender. Dance houses and amusement resorts existed in many nineteenth-century cities. But they were considered immoral and vulgar by most Victorians, although some working-class people, especially German Americans, viewed them as perfectly acceptable entertainment. To the middle class, waltzing and other couple dancing needed to be carefully controlled and chaperoned, because it brought women and men into such close proximity. By the turn of the century, however, commercial dance halls had sprung up in the tenement districts of such cities as New York, Chicago, Baltimore, and Philadelphia. "Dance mad" working women donned their best dresses and flocked to these urban night spots—even after a long day of work. There they interacted with men in bold new ways: accepting dates with unfamiliar men, drinking beer and cocktails, flirting, and dancing the latest steps to the syncopated rhythms of ragtime. The new dances carried outrageous names—turkey trot, bunny hug, grizzly bear, shimmy, Charlie Chaplin wiggle, and Charleston—and entailed even more outrageous steps. Originating in African American culture and performed initially in the "low" resorts of San Francisco and other cities, these dances were energetic, intimate, filled with sexual innuendo, and immensely popular with working girls and their male partners.

By 1912, the dance craze had spread to the middle class. Until the 1910s, most commercial nightspots were considered male territory, although respectable middle-class women, escorted by gentlemen, began to go to public restaurants. In the 1910s, cabarets and other nightclubs began to offer dining, dancing, and shows for urban sophisticates of both sexes. Dancing masters such as Irene and Vernon Castle tamed the new movements into elegant yet expressive dances, and middle-class

nightclubbers quickly adopted their version of the "Castle Walk," two-step, and tango. Many women not only emulated Irene Castle's dancing but copied her modern style of dress and appearance; she was one of the first well-known figures to bob her hair.

The Movies

Women also turned to the movies for entertainment and insight into fashion and appearance. In the early twentieth century, films were shown in vaudeville houses and small storefront theaters known as nickelodeons. Initially located in working-class tenement districts, movie theaters by 1910 were attracting a more diverse, middle-class audience. From the beginning, working-class and immigrant women went to the movies: Single women went with girlfriends or a "date," and mothers gathered up their children and went to a show. Middle-class women soon followed. In the 1920s, the movie business became a two-billion-dollar industry, turning out a steady stream of feature films and a dazzling array of movie stars. Exhibitors built opulent "picture palaces" in the central amusement districts of cities, while nearly every town and neighborhood boasted its own theater. By 1929, an average of eighty million Americans attended the movies every week.

The movies played a crucial role in creating and popularizing new notions of gender. Audiences scrutinized movie stars such as Mary Pickford, Clara Bow, Douglas Fairbanks, and Rudolph Valentino on the screen and followed their lives in "fanzines" like *Photoplay* and *Modern Screen*. Pickford's self-conscious image as a working girl enjoying her youth, health, and independence symbolized to many the New Woman of the 1910s, while her leading man Douglas Fairbanks conveyed

the white-collar athleticism and clean-cut masculinity that had become an ideal among men. In the twenties, such flapper movies as *Our Dancing Daughters* and *It* explored the possibilities and problems of the modern young woman: Could women who stayed up late, flirted with men, and danced wildly at parties still be virtuous and "true"?

However viewers understood the message of these movies, they were attentive to every detail. Hollywood became a new source of fashion, and the movies could change popular taste virtually overnight. When Joan Crawford appeared in the 1932 film *Letty Lynton* wearing a white ruffled dress with big puffed sleeves, women flocked to retailers demanding the new style. The images on the screen—larger than life with the use of close-up photography—provided viewers with a shared repertoire of so-called masculine and feminine ways of dressing, moving, and gesturing. In a study on movies and conduct published in 1933, researchers found that women learned how to pose seductively, flirt, and kiss by watching the movies. When glamorous stars appeared with eyes heavily made up or cigarette in hand, women followed suit.

Joan Crawford as Letty Lynton, 1932. *(Courtesy of the Academy of Motion Picture Arts and Sciences)*

At the same time, movies reinforced trends that were already taking place, such as the growing acceptance of women smoking in public. In the nineteenth century, tobacco was largely reserved for men, so cigar smoke and spittoons marked a room or public place as male territory. In the early 1900s, daring women smoked in secret, or took a few cautious puffs in public, but most viewed smoking as unladylike and improper. Cigarette companies' persistent advertising led many men to switch to cigarettes by the 1920s; women who embraced ''modernity'' began smoking them, too. The ritual of lighting up and smoking took on new meaning in the public realm of mixed-sex socializing and romance.

Estimating Beauty

The costumes and customs of the teens and twenties suggest the distance between the ''modern'' woman and her Victorian sister. Clothing and appearance conveyed a sense of independence, physical movement, and expressiveness—a sense that was affirmed in the leisure pursuits of the era. Nevertheless, this modernity had another side that contradicted women's new-found freedom: Women in the twenties were encouraged to see themselves as sexual objects whose primary concern was to attract a man. Selling soap, beauty aids, deodorants, and mouthwash, advertisers

Mrs. A. S. Guimaraes wore this two-piece swimsuit of black and white wool in 1922. Form-fitting knit suits allowed women to swim in earnest rather than merely ''bathe'' in the water.

beauty contests of this period. Beauty contests were held in spas and seaside resorts in the late 1800s, but they became widespread in the twentieth century. Newspapers, civic organizations, and neighborhoods would frequently sponsor competitions to choose the most beautiful woman. In 1921, the first Miss America contest was held in Atlantic City, New Jersey, with a parade and pageant on the beach. Judges chose Margaret Gorman of Washington, D.C., who bested eight other contestants. The next year fifty-eight contestants joined the pageant. Influential hotels in Atlantic City complained that their patrons objected to the display of semi-nude female bodies, so the pageant closed from 1927 to 1935.

Do you think they're all certified virgins?

Bennett Cerf, judging the Miss America Pageant, 1958

To make the pageant more respectable, its sponsors later dropped the term ''Bathing Beauty'' and, in 1937, added a talent competition. Contestants were expected to have high moral standards and represent America's ''ideal.'' However, they still displayed themselves in bathing suits and high-heeled shoes.

But a woman did not need to enter a beauty pageant to feel that her appearance was being judged. She could hear comments about her looks when she stepped into the public realm. And she often had more than hostile words to fear. On the job, in factories, stores, and offices, women faced harassment from employers, co-workers, and customers. Sexual harassment limited women's position in the workforce and maintained male privilege and control. It curtailed women's independence by making it unpleasant or even dangerous for women to frequent public places without a male escort. Although most women in this period had no choice but to endure this behavior, women office workers in Washington, D.C. formed the

played on women's fears that they would remain ''old maids'' and encouraged competition between women for ''Mr. Right.''

Women's costume also contained a dual message. Swimwear changed decisively in the twenties, as active swimming, not just bathing or beach-sitting, became popular among women. Most put aside skirted bathing costumes and put on knitted suits modeled on those worn by men. These form-fitting suits allowed greater movement and freedom to female swimmers, but they also frankly revealed the shape of women's bodies to male onlookers, who judged what they saw with stares, whistles, and colorful commentary.

This public ritual of male voyeurism and female exhibitionism was most explicit in the

There she is, Miss America of 1921, Margaret Gorman. Contestants competed in high heels and bathing suits on the Atlantic City boardwalk. *(Courtesy of the Miss America Pageant)*

Anti-Flirt club in the 1920s to campaign against harassment.

The common depiction of the twenties' woman as fancy-free and liberated belies the complex reality of women's lives at this time. Many women could not afford all the clothes and accessories deemed necessary to the modern woman; others, because of religious beliefs or cultural traditions, rejected the new emphasis on style and social freedom. With the stock market crash of 1929 and the ensuing Great Depression, the popular image of the flapper crumbled.

Depression ravaged the economy of the United States. By 1933, one-quarter of the American workforce was unemployed. Families lost their homes, their farms, and their livelihoods. High levels of unemployment and the scarcity of income meant that consumer spending on clothing was curtailed. Although women continued to buy face powder and lipstick—the cosmetics industry was considered "depression-proof"—most made do with fewer new purchases, wore hand-me-downs, and updated their wardrobes by sewing new details on old clothes. Moreover, the Depression fostered greater resistance to women's wage labor and independence. Working women, especially working wives, were accused of taking away jobs from men, even though most women labored in sex-segregated positions. Married women who were public school teachers, for example, were fired in a number of cities. Many people worried about what would happen to men's "natural" authority in marriage if men were unemployed and women took up the slack by working. Fearing gender role reversal, many sociologists and psychologists urged women to strengthen their roles as wives and homemakers and subordinate themselves to their husbands. Women continued to care deeply about fashion and style—reading fashion magazines and watching the glamorous stars of the silver screen—but the promise of "modernity" evaporated in the trying conditions of the Depression.

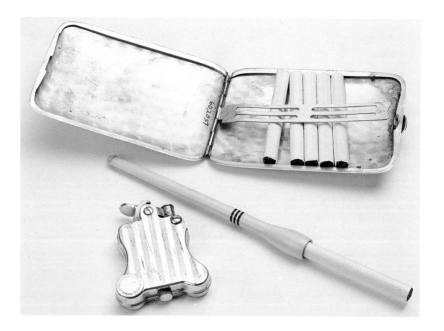

Once a male prerogative, smoking became the rage among modern women of the 1920s, for whom cigarettes symbolized glamour and sophistication.

(Right) Unisex clothes of the 1960s: sandals, jeans, old Navy shirt with "strike" stencil, bandana, and jewelry.

The social rules for appearance have changed frequently and dramatically since 1940. Changes in dress have marked the period of national emergency and mobilization during World War II, the years of social conformity in the fifties, and the era of upheaval and rebellion in the sixties. Recent decades have seen efforts by the fashion industry, mass media, and others to endorse ideals of proper masculine and feminine appearance, as well as direct challenges to stultifying fashionable images and constraining gender roles. Conformity and contention have been the themes of our times.

For women, the definition of "femininity" during World War II was ambiguous and contradictory. More than six million women—including many wives and mothers—went out to work for the first time during the war. Wartime conditions encouraged women to step away from their domestic roles, and many moved into jobs traditionally reserved for men. Most of them took clerical and factory jobs in war-related industries. After some initial hesitation, government and business used advertising and radio to encourage women to enter war work. To promote women's employment, the War Manpower Commission urged a policy of equal pay for male and female workers. In 1942, Congress passed legislation providing some support for child-care facilities. Most women felt it was their patriotic duty to support the war effort, but they were also attracted to the higher wages of traditionally male jobs, as well as the new skills they were learning.

The image of "Rosie the Riveter" powerfully symbolized women's new roles during the war, but most people saw these roles as temporary. Government and business stressed that these positions were for the duration only. As a result, women rarely received equal pay or found adequate child care. Women were reminded of the importance of femininity on the home front, however masculine their new jobs seemed.

Women working in shipbuilding, armaments factories, and other war-related industries frequently wore the same clothing on the job as men: sturdy overalls or trousers, hard hats, tool belts, and thick-soled shoes. But many women who wore pants also wore fancy hair styles, heavy makeup, or feminine underwear. Advertisers, government spokesmen, and others agreed that women should be careful to "stay feminine." Lipstick, for example,

No lipstick—ours or anyone else's—will win the war. But it symbolizes one of the reasons why we are fighting . . . the precious right of women to be feminine and lovely—under any circumstances.

"War, Women and Lipstick," Tangee Lipsticks ad, **Photoplay** *magazine, September 1943*

Wartime femininity.

became an important symbol of femininity during World War II. In July 1942, the U.S. government's War Production Board limited the manufacture of beauty supplies because of the need to conserve the metal used in cosmetics packaging. In October, after a groundswell of complaints from women, the board changed its mind. Lipstick was considered important for maintaining the morale of women and men. According to one lipstick manufacturer, lipstick symbolized what American men were fighting for.

Women continued to see fashion as an important part of femininity—some purchased attractive new clothes with their high wages, for example—but being stylish proved difficult in a period of shortages and rationing. The "inverted triangle" shape and broad shoulders of the 1930s

were on their way out of fashion when the war started and the U.S. government stepped in. To conserve textiles, clothing, and leather for both military and civilian populations, the War Production Board deemed it necessary to counteract the wastefulness of ever-changing styles. It set up regulations to "freeze" fashions and prevent existing clothes from becoming obsolete. These regulations, observed Stanley Marcus of Neiman-Marcus, who headed the women's and children's section of the board, "effectively prevented any change of skirt length downward and blocked any extreme new sleeve or collar development, which might have encouraged women to discard their existing clothes."[13]

The shortage of silk for stockings during World War II led companies to market makeup for women's legs; women painted seams up the back. *(Courtesy of Bonne Bell Cosmetics)*

Women filled in for men not only in the workplace, but in many other ways as well. When the war threatened major-league baseball, Philip Wrigley founded the All American Girls Baseball League in 1943 to keep the ball parks open and to entertain war workers. At its peak, the league had 160 women under contract. The women were skillful players, but Wrigley worried about the "masculine" image long associated with women's softball. He set up rigid rules for dress and behavior that established the players' femininity as the first priority. Players wore skirts—never slacks or shorts—on and off the field. Beauty consultants such as Helena Rubinstein gave the players tips on appearance, and chaperones accompanied them everywhere.

For most men, the requirements of masculinity were clear during the war. It was manly to shoulder the burdens of national defense, in or out of the armed services. The short-haired, clean-cut look associated with the military expressed a man or boy's belief in these values. Men wore jackets that had shoulder pads and narrowed at the waist in an inverted triangle shape. Originating in the 1930s in women's fashion, this style became popular for both sexes in the 1940s. During the war it came to be seen as a military look.

But a small number of American men adopted an appearance that expressed a dissenting idea of masculinity. Excluded by age, ethnic background, race, or poverty from mainstream society, some young Mexican Americans, or *pachucos*, and some young Black men wore "zoot suits" in the early 1940s. The zoot suit had "a killer diller coat, with a drape shape, reat pleats, and shoulders padded like a lunatic's cell."[14] What did the zoot suit mean?

These suits contrasted sharply with American men's accepted style of dress and were

emblems of their wearers' difference and alienation from mainstream American culture. The huge, baggy zoot suit violated the War Production Board's restrictions on the use of fabric in wartime. Together with the "Argentine" ducktail haircut worn by Mexican American youth, they proclaimed their wearers' ethnicity, energy, and status as outsiders. Zoot suits expressed an alternative ideal of masculinity to that embodied by the clean-cut soldier. There were also some zoot suit girls, who wore the "killer diller coat" with short skirts and patterned stockings. These Mexican American girls departed

A young man in Los Angeles displays the "killer-diller" coat, baggy pants, and long chain of the zoot suiter, 1943. *(Courtesy of UPI/Bettmann Newsphotos)*

from mainstream definitions of propriety and femininity. Through their dress, they expressed their ethnicity, class, and gender identity. To most white Americans, zoot suiters and their ''girls'' seemed unpatriotic. In 1943, sailors stationed in Los Angeles rioted against Mexican youths, tearing the zoot suits from them. Similar riots followed in Texas, Arizona, Detroit, and New York, fueled by race and class tensions.

After the War

When the war came to an end in 1945, Americans hoped to return to some semblance of normal life after years of economic hardship, geographical dislocation, and the loss of family and friends. But what was ''normal life''? Reasserting traditional concepts of masculinity and femininity helped many Americans feel more stable and secure in a changed world. As soldiers and sailors returned home to look for work, women were laid off from their high-paying factory jobs. They found positions in the service and clerical sector of the economy, the ''pink-collar'' ghetto where most women work. Women were urged to find fulfillment not in work but in the role of homemaker and mother. And reversing a decades-long decline in the birth rate, women after the war had babies—lots of them. Returning veterans and other men eagerly looked for jobs that would reinstate them as chief breadwinner of the family. The benefits of the G.I. bill rewarded their sacrifice during the war with opportunities for upward mobility by providing low-interest loans for higher education and housing. As Americans moved to the suburbs in droves, family life took on a specific cast—Mom, Dad, and the kids—a configuration sociologists, psychologists, and other

experts agreed was ''natural'' and fulfilling to men and women.

To be masculine in the fifties meant being a mature and responsible breadwinner who married young and diligently supported the family. Although men worked in a variety of jobs, a growing percentage found positions in the postwar years as salaried white-collar workers and managers. The ''man in the grey flannel suit'' signified the world of the modern corporation. With this suit, a button-down collar shirt, conservative tie, and leather briefcase, Dad sought to climb the ladder of business success, along with millions of other middle-class

Soldier into civilian: masculine roles and options for appearance in the postwar era were suggested in this *New Yorker* cover. Cover-drawing by Alajalov; © 1945, 1983. The New Yorker Magazine, Inc. By special permission. All rights reserved.

The Halle Bros. Co.
CLEVELAND

men. The suit became a symbol of the conformity and facelessness required of men who worked in regimented, bureaucratic, and hierarchical organizations. Some men wondered whether they had become interchangeable in the work world. They also wondered whether the rewards of work were worthwhile. Concerned about heart disease and work-related stress, doctors and others advised men to resist social pressures toward money-making and success.

After the disruptions of the war years, and in the face of often unsatisfying jobs, many men sought individuality and fulfillment in the private sphere. At home and at leisure, men frequently wore exuberant colors and patterns—such as Hawaiian shirts and checked golfing pants—that expressed their sense of individual taste. The ''do-it-yourself'' movement of the fifties encouraged men to spend their leisure fixing up the house and yard, while marriage manuals counseled togetherness and companionship as the route to a happy marriage. On television, Dad was sometimes a powerful figure whose parental authority and role as advisor to children eclipsed Mom's. But there was another TV image of Dad that perhaps reflected many men's fears of their new involvement in the household: the laughable, ineffectual husband, henpecked by his wife and mocked by his children.

Mom was supposed to be a contented homebody. As one Harvard senior in 1955 described the wife he wanted: ''The marriage must be the most important thing that ever happened to her.''[15] That, and children. From the late 1940s through the 1950s, America's birthrate soared, as many young couples had three, four, and five children. Child-care experts told mothers that they had to stay home to raise their children. Many women did choose home and family over careers, a fact *Life* magazine noted enthusiastically in 1956: ''Of all the accomplishments of the American woman, one she brings off with the most spectacular success is having babies.''[16] Postwar affluence made it possible for some to try to put into practice the era's new romantic ideal of family life.

Mom was responsible for the house and kids when Dad left early in the morning and returned late at night. With convenience foods and electric appliances, new consumer products supposedly made her work easier, although studies show that she spent as much time performing housework and child care as her mother did. Higher standards of cleanliness meant more laundry and vacuuming, and women's magazines urged her to expand her culinary repertoire. Suburban sprawl meant she spent hours

Femininity reborn: a popular version of women's ''New Look'' after the war.

driving to the grocery store, mall, school, and railway station. But all this made women happy, noted *Life* magazine. Feminism was a "dead issue."[17]

For women of the late forties and fifties, the fashionable shape became the hourglass silhouette, heralded by Christian Dior's "New Look." With its pinched-in waist and billowing skirt, the New Look symbolized to many the heightened femininity of the 1950s, particularly in contrast to men's fashion—the inverted triangle shape emphasizing broad shoulders and narrowed torso continued to be popular among men after the war. At the same time, women combined many roles and needed many changes of costume, from sportswear to evening dress. Mom might wear pedal pushers— brightly colored pants cut for women—for housework and leisure. She wore smart shirtwaists to shop, lunch with friends, and attend meetings of the PTA or other organizations. When Dad took her out at night, she transformed herself into an alluring partner, wearing a sequined gown or low-cut sheath.

Many women chose to make marriage and children their priority during the fifties. But for more and more families, the good life was possible

Any haircut you want, as long as it's short. A barber shop display poster, 1950s.

Dad goes Hawaiian: color and pattern became permissible for men's leisure clothes in the 1950s.

only because Mom worked a "double shift," doing the housework and childrearing within the home and working for wages outside the home. And among those who chose to stay home, a growing number of women—especially those with higher education—found their lives unfulfilling. In 1963, Betty Friedan published *The Feminine Mystique*, which described the depression and malaise of some housewives who lacked a sense of focus or meaning in their suburban lives.

Some men, too, felt a sense of unease. They worried about living a depersonalized life, reduced to machines in their work. A tiny minority of men left behind responsibility to job, women, and children to roam across the country, seek meaningful experiences, and sometimes write about them. This group came to be called the "Beat Generation." For the majority, the ideas of the "Beats" provided only a romantic vision of escape from the daily grind. But the dissatisfaction and frustration underlying ordinary men's interest in the Beat movement were real. Popular culture reflected these concerns. When Hugh Hefner first published *Playboy* in 1953, he argued against the "traps" of marriage, alimony, and "money-hungry women" in general. Bachelorhood was touted as a lifestyle of freedom and adventure: A "playboy" could escape from the role of breadwinner and husband without meeting the hostility that many Americans directed toward those suspected of homosexuality. Hollywood picked up the idea of male rebellion and offered its own images of romantic masculinity in such screen stars as James Dean and Marlon Brando.

Rebelliousness could also be seen among the nation's youth. Many teen-age boys wore the clean-cut, "khaki" look, but some adopted blue jeans and ducktail haircuts as the insignia of a new youth culture. Middle-class parents and teachers worried that their children were being infected with the styles of dress and music identified with lower-class culture. Did comic books, TV, and rock-and-roll influence children more than parents, school, and church combined? Worried about the threat of juvenile delinquency, many schools instituted tough dress codes, banning jeans on boys and tight sweaters, heavy makeup and short skirts for girls.

The Sixties

The expression of unrest became a torrent of protest in the 1960s. In the early fifties, Black Americans had challenged southern "Jim Crow" laws that had established separate schools, jobs, buses, and other public facilities for "white" and "colored." By the 1960s, growing numbers of whites also became aware of inequality and poverty in America. White youth, often from well-to-do families, began to reject the consumerism and social apathy that characterized their culture's ideals of success. Some became active in support of Black rights and other political movements. Many Americans, Black and white, expressed their new attitudes through dress and appearance. Costume conveyed a wide range of political meanings in the sixties.

Blacks had long felt the impact of white Americans' standards of beauty. Although Black entrepreneurs had developed beauty products aimed specifically at Black women and men as early as the late nineteenth century, some products and advertising assumed that "nappy" hair was less attractive than straight hair and that dark skin was less beautiful than light skin. African Americans rejected these standards in the 1960s. The "Black Is Beautiful" movement celebrated Black appearance

Question: What are you rebelling against? Answer: "What've ya got?"
Marlon Brando, The Wild One, *1954*

and fostered new ideals for African American femininity and masculinity. As the civil rights movement shifted its emphasis from integration to separatist goals, Blacks drew on African cultures for such clothing as the *dashiki*, a colorful and richly patterned shirt or blouse that symbolized an alternative identity and separate heritage. Both men and women rejected hair straightening for the "Afro" or "natural"—a symbol of Black pride. The "Black Is Beautiful" movement changed many Blacks' sense of themselves and influenced the perceptions of many white Americans as well.

College students and other young people used a variety of clothes as symbols for political protest and as cultural markers dividing generations. Young Americans in tie-dyed shirts, embroidered cotton blouses, jeans, T-shirts and other inexpensive clothes pointedly ignored the dictates of high fashion. To an alarming extent they chose not to buy products offered by the fashion industry.

Young men of the sixties violated long-standing conventions of male appearance. Whether

The film *Easy Rider* depicted the clash of two different concepts of masculinity in 1969. As in the movie, long-haired young men frequently stirred suspicions of homosexuality and anti-Americanism among their elders in the sixties. *(Courtesy of the Academy of Motion Picture Arts and Sciences)*

they wore blue jeans and work shirts, which imitated the dress of the working class, or brightly patterned clothes and bold colors, their costume visibly expressed their opposition to middle-class standards of decorum, conformity, and success. Even more important, many young men abandoned an important gender symbol: short hair.

Short hair in the fifties had conveyed an image of staunch masculinity in keeping with an era anxious about the Cold War and military might. A long-haired man was considered effeminate or homosexual. For sixties' youth, wearing long hair symbolized opposition to the older generation's authority and standards of masculinity. Fathers who had fought in World War II and had worked in the 1950s for material comfort and social mobility saw

their sons rejecting their examples. Worn by protesters against the Vietnam War, long hair also symbolized the rejection of Cold War politics and the military.

Young women's clothing challenged the assumptions of the older generation as well. In the mid-sixties, miniskirts became fashionable, and teen-age girls took to the style with a passion. Like the flapper style of the twenties, the "mini" symbolized physical movement and energy. The boyish, leggy look made popular by Twiggy and other top models put a premium on youth and slenderness. To many, the miniskirt represented the sexual revolution. Parents and school officials struggled with girls over inches of fabric, fearful that the mini spelled sexual promiscuity.

Dashiki, 1970; Black power jewelry, early 1970s. *(Courtesy of Sandra and Spencer Crew)*

By the late sixties, many women had begun to wear jeans, the style of their male friends. Bought at Army-Navy or other outlet stores, jeans made for boys and men found their way onto girls' and women's bodies. Worn with a T-shirt, jeans made a unisex uniform for youth. By dressing alike, young men and women denied that gender made as much difference to their identities as age did. But these gestures caused confusion and spelled rebellion among their elders. As many young Americans abandoned their parents' two most important gender symbols—short hair for males, skirts for females—parents complained that "you can't tell the girls from the boys." The new clothing style led to conflicts with school authorities, parents, and supporters of the Vietnam War.

Fashion soon became a target for the nascent feminist movement, as women renewed the struggle for legal, economic, and social equality in the late 1960s. In 1968, feminists picketed the Miss America Pageant in Atlantic City, New Jersey. In a dramatic protest, they threw symbols of women's oppression into a trash can: bras, girdles, curlers, high heels, makeup, dishrags, diapers, and steno pads. Protesters objected to restrictive clothing and argued that the fashion and beauty industries cast women as sexual objects. Many feminists stopped wearing bras, nylon stockings, and makeup, shaving their legs, and plucking their eyebrows. Women who flouted such fashion rules often were subject to insults on the street or problems at work. But rejecting fashion was a gesture of self-acceptance. By refusing to exaggerate artificially the physical differences between women and men, feminists challenged conventional concepts of femininity and masculinity.

Supporters of women's liberation

Symbols of women's oppression? Feminists "trashed" items like these by throwing them into a garbage can. The demonstration took place on the Atlantic City boardwalk at the 1968 Miss America Pageant.

With the rise of the feminist movement, some women abandoned conventions of feminine appearance.

became known as "bra burners," even though feminists never actually burned a bra in a public protest. The term implicitly compared feminists to draft-card burners who refused to support the war in Southeast Asia. It also marked them as "promiscuous." Just as people in the nineteenth century used the bloomer costume to discredit the women's rights movement, the myth of bra-burning in the sixties trivialized the ideal of liberation.

In the late 1960s and early 1970s, gay men and lesbians created an increasingly visible movement to secure gay rights and assert "gay pride." Many lesbian women took part in the feminist rejection of fashion and the traditional restrictions on women's appearance. In the seventies, many gay men adopted a more conventional masculine look. While straight men had adopted longer hair, bright colors, and other elements associated with femininity, gay men turned to short hair and muscular bodies to counter the popular public image of homosexual men as effeminate.

Do Your Own Thing

How did the fashion industry respond to these challenges? Some innovative designers, like Rudi Gernreich, suggested clothes for the future. In 1970, he proposed clothing that differed with people's age but not with their gender. Old people, he predicted, would wear gowns that covered their bodies, making men and women indistinguishable. Young men and women, who would want to show off their bodies, would wear identical, revealing apparel. Gernreich's sense that generational differences were naturally more significant than gender differences—and hence should be visually underlined—reflected the ideas of the 1960s. He raised on the level of high style the

possibility that some youth had raised in their daily lives through "low" style: Dress could be used to signal and possibly create changes in the way men and women related with one another and felt about themselves.

Gernreich's imaginative response was atypical. The fashion industry struck back, fearful of the trend toward "anti-fashion." Clothing manufacturers made jeans for women, offering new styles cut to emphasize women's hips and attaching designer labels that could add a cachet to the product. Worn with high heels and makeup, women's jeans no longer symbolized rebellion against fashion and femininity. Bras were redesigned and marketed as less restrictive and more "natural." Cosmetics and hair care companies advertised products containing herbs and other organic ingredients, touting their healthful, natural qualities. The dominant culture adapted and co-opted the challenge of the counter-culture, turning what had once seemed subversive into marketable consumer products. Jeans, long hair, and other styles lost the rebellious meanings given them by hippies and dissatisfied youth. "Do your own thing" was no longer a revolutionary slogan: It was a fashion statement.

Today the fashion and beauty industry advises each of us to be ourselves, to emphasize our individuality through clothing and appearance. The possibilities for doing so have expanded tremendously in recent years. Yet individuality remains powerfully shaped by ideal images about how we should appear as gendered beings. In the 1980s, for example, the fitness craze has fostered the image of a fitter, healthier body. Yet this ideal carries different messages for women and men. As in the 1890s, many men are obsessed with the appearance of personal power and strength that muscles convey. Huge muscles for women, however, are generally considered ugly or bizarre. Women's fitness is closely

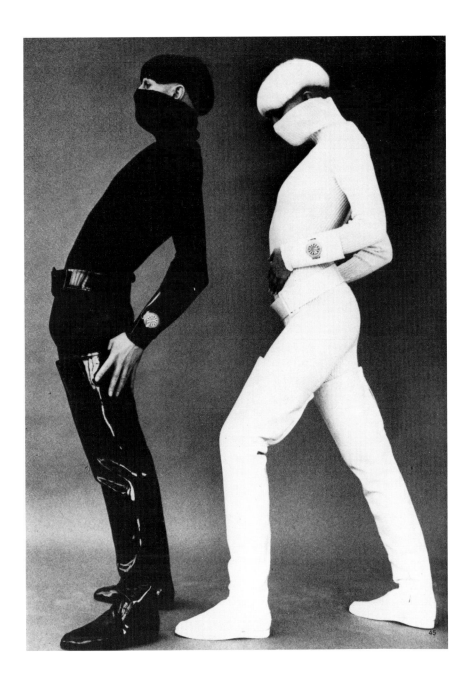

linked to achieving a slim, youthful figure; for some, this ideal leads to an obsession with dieting and weight loss, often with devastating consequences. Women and men are still required to distinguish themselves visually from one another.

Who wears the pants? This question has caused a great deal of conflict over the years, largely because pants have symbolized the privileged status accorded men in American society. Today women wear pants for many occasions, a sign of expanding

Rudi Gernreich's unisex clothing augured a world without gender distinctions. *(Courtesy of Oreste F. Pucciani from the estate of Rudi Gernreich)*

freedom and participation in activities once reserved for men. Yet pants and skirts retain their powerful symbolism. In business and politics, the older rules of dressing still apply; few women managers, administrators, or politicians wear pants to the office. Successful women continue to signify their femininity, however far up the ladder they have climbed. And although some designers have tried to introduce high-style skirts for men, few men would consider being associated with this symbol of femininity and inferiority. ''Who wears the *skirts*'' continues to be a self-evident question to most of us.

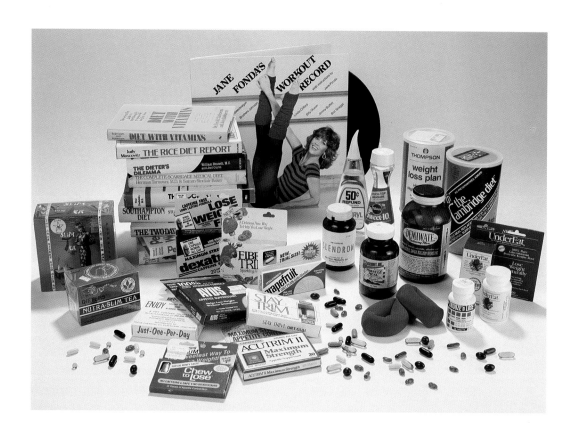

Products promoting an ideal body shape of the 1980s.
(Handweights courtesy of Genese Kerns)

NOTES

1. George Washington quoted in Arthur Schlesinger, "The Aristocrats," in *The Birth of the Nation: A Portrait of the American People on the Eve of Independence* (Boston, 1968), 135.

2. Thorstein Veblen, *The Theory of the Leisure Class* (1899; rpt. New York, 1975), 149, 172.

3. *Harper's Magazine*, 1857, quoted in Lois Banner, *American Beauty* (Chicago, 1984), 95–96.

4. Mary Tillotson, *Progress versus Fashion*, 1983, quoted in Lois Banner, *American Beauty*, 96.

5. Ernest Thompson Seton, *Handbook* of the Boy Scouts of America, 1910, quoted in Peter Filene, *Him/Her/Self: Sex Roles in Modern America*, 2nd ed. (Baltimore, 1986), 95.

6. *Independent Magazine*, 11 November 1909, quoted in Benjamin G. Rader, *American Sports: From the Age of Folk Games to the Age of Spectators* (Englewood Cliffs, N.J., 1983), 148.

7. Margaret Deland, "The Change in the Feminine Ideal," *Atlantic Monthly* 105 (March 1910): 289–302.

8. *New York World* quoted in Martha Banta, *Imaging American Women: Idea and Ideals in Cultural History* (New York, 1987), 83–85.

9. Dr. M.L. Holbrook, *Parturition Without Pain: A Code of Directions for Escaping from the Primal Curse* (New York, 1882), 14–15, quoted in Charles Rosenberg and Carroll Smith-Rosenberg, "The Female Animal: Medical and Biological Views of Woman and Her Role in 19th-Century America," *Journal of American History* 60 (September 1973): 335.

10. *The Woman's Home Companion*, 1908, quoted in Valerie Steele, "Dressing for Work," in Claudia Brush Kidwell and Valerie Steele, eds., *Men and Women: Dressing the Part* (Washington, D.C., 1989), 84.

11. Elizabeth Hillard Ragan, "One Secretary as per Specifications," *Saturday Evening Post* 203 (12 December 1931): 10, quoted in Margery W. Davies, *Woman's Place Is at the Typewriter: Office Work and Office Workers, 1870–1930* (Philadelphia, 1982), 153.

12. The quote is from Carol Kregloh, unpublished ms. on *Godey's Lady's Book*. A 1902 writer in the New York *Times* saw shingled hair as "a token of masculinity" incompatible with women's "long-haired ways."

13. Quoted in Claudia Brush Kidwell, "Gender Symbols or Fashionable Details?" in Kidwell and Steele, eds., *Men and Women*, 137.

14. Stuart Cosgrove, "The Zoot Suit and Style Warfare," *History Workshop Journal* 18 (Autumn 1984): 77–91.

15. Quoted in Sara Evans, *Personal Politics: The Roots of Women's Liberation in the Civil Rights Movement and the New Left* (New York, 1979), 8.

16. *Life*, 24 December 1956, quoted in Evans, *Personal Politics*, 1.

17. Evans, *Personal Politics*, 4.

78

BIBLIOGRAPHY

Lois Banner. *American Beauty*. Chicago, 1984.

Martha Banta. *Imaging American Women: Idea and Ideals in Cultural History*. New York, 1987.

Susan Brownmiller. *Femininity*. New York, 1984.

Kim Chernin. *The Obsession: Reflections on the Tyranny of Slenderness*. New York, 1981.

Stuart Cosgrove. ''The Zoot Suit and Style Warfare.'' *History Workshop Journal* 18 (Autumn 1984): 77–91.

Margery W. Davies. *Woman's Place Is at the Typewriter: Office Work and Office Workers, 1870–1930*. Philadelphia, 1982.

Barbara Ehrenreich. *The Hearts of Men: American Dreams and the Flight from Commitment*. Garden City, N.Y., 1983.

Sara Evans. *Personal Politics: The Roots of Women's Liberation in the Civil Rights Movement and the New Left*. New York, 1979.

Peter Filene. *Him/Her/Self: Sex Roles in Modern America*. 2nd ed. Baltimore, 1986.

Paula Giddings. *When and Where I Enter: The Impact of Black Women on Race and Sex in America*. New York, 1984.

Sherna Berger Gluck. *Rosie the Riveter Revisited: Women, the War, and Social Change*. Boston, 1987.

Linda Gordon. *Woman's Body, Woman's Right: A Social History of Birth Control in America*. New York, 1976.

Elliott Gorn. *The Manly Art: Bare Knuckle Prize Fighting in America*. Ithaca, N.Y., 1986.

Harvey Green. *Fit for America: Health, Fitness, Sport and American Society*. New York, 1986.

Karen Halttunen. *Confidence Men and Painted Women*. New Haven, 1982.

Anne Hollander. *Seeing Through Clothes*. New York, 1975.

Alice Kessler-Harris. *Out to Work*. New York, 1982.

Claudia B. Kidwell. ''Women's Bathing and Swimming Costume in the United States.'' Washington, D.C., 1968.

Claudia B. Kidwell and Margaret C. Christman. *Suiting Everyone: The Democratization of Clothing in America*. Washington, D.C., 1974.

Claudia Brush Kidwell and Valerie Steele, eds. *Men and Women: Dressing the Part*. Washington, D.C., 1989.

Gerda Lerner. *The Majority Finds Its Past*. New York, 1979.

Marcia Millman. *Such a Pretty Face: Being Fat in America*. New York, 1980.

Robin Morgan, ed. *Sisterhood Is Powerful: An Anthology of Writings from the Women's Liberation Movement*. New York, 1970.

Jo Paoletti. ''Ridicule and Role Models as Factors in American Men's Fashion Change, 1880–1910.'' *Costume: The Journal of the Costume Society* 19 (1985): 121–134.

Kathy Peiss. *Cheap Amusements: Working Women and Leisure in Turn-of-the-Century New York*. Philadelphia, 1986.

Gwendolyn Keita Robinson. *Crowning Glory: An Historical Analysis of the Afro-American Beauty Industry and Tradition*. Urbana, Ill., forthcoming.

Mary P. Ryan. *Womanhood in America*. 3d. ed. New York, 1983.

Robert A. Smith. *A Social History of the Bicycle*. New York, 1972.

Carroll Smith-Rosenberg. *Disorderly Conduct: Visions of Gender in Victorian America*. New York, 1985.

Valerie Steele. *Fashion and Eroticism: Ideals of Feminine Beauty from the Victorian Era to the Jazz Age*. New York, 1985.

Valerie Steele. ''The Social and Political Significance of Macaroni Fashion.'' *Costume* 19 (1985): 94–109.

Susan Strasser. *Never Done: A History of American Housework*. New York, 1982.

Thorstein Veblen. *The Theory of the Leisure Class*. 1899. Reprinted, New York, 1975.

Elizabeth Wilson. *Adorned in Dreams: Fashion and Modernity*. Berkeley, 1987.

All object photographs are by Dane A. Penland, Division of Printing and Photographic Services, Smithsonian Institution, with the following exceptions: The photographs on pages 20 (padded vest) and 27 are by Richard Strauss; those on pages 13, 14, and 17 are by Jeffrey Ploskonka; the photograph on page 20 (1880s corset) is by Alfred F. Harrell.

All objects are the property of the Smithsonian Institution unless otherwise noted.

Men and Women: A History of Costume, Gender, and Power was printed by Schneidereith and Sons, Baltimore, Maryland. The text was set by BG Composition, Baltimore, Maryland, in Garamond Book Condensed. It was printed on 80 lb. Warren Lustro Offset Enamel dull text; the cover was printed on 10 pt. Warren Lusterkote cover.